Challenge

Science

Mark Edwards

**Age 11–14
Years 7–9**
Key Stage 3

Introduction

One of the most powerful things about Science is its ability to explain many different things using just a few ideas. This book challenges you to use your scientific knowledge to explore all sorts of different situations. The questions are not only designed to give you a thorough revision of all the topics from the Key Stage 3 National Curriculum but also to extend your knowledge and understanding and to get you thinking like a scientist.

Each topic begins with a few practice questions. These introduce you to the ideas and the scientific words that you need to use in the later questions. If you struggle with the practice questions then either move to a new topic or go back to your revision guide (try our *Revise KS3* series) The 'challenge' questions range in difficulty. Some are standard questions that you might see in an exam. Others encourage you to look up further information. A few are designed to really stretch your mind. Don't worry: if all else fails, there are detailed answers at the back of the book. Good luck!

Hachette UK's policy is to use papers that are natural, renewable and recyclable products and made from wood grown in sustainable forests. The logging and manufacturing processes are expected to conform to the environmental regulations of the country of origin.

Orders: please contact Bookpoint Ltd, 130 Milton Park, Abingdon, Oxon OX14 4SB. Telephone: +44 (0)1235 827720. Fax: +44 (0)1235 400454. Lines are open 9.00a.m.–5.00p.m., Monday to Saturday, with a 24-hour message answering service. Visit our website at www.hoddereducation.co.uk.

© Mark Edwards 2013
First published in 2007 exclusively for WHSmith by
Hodder Education
An Hachette UK Company
338 Euston Road
London NW1 3BH

This second edition first published in 2013 exclusively for WHSmith
Teacher's tips © Alison Popperwell 2013
Impression number   10 9 8 7 6 5 4 3 2 1
Year   2018 2017 2016 2015 2014 2013

Cover illustration by Oxford Designers and Illustrators Ltd
Illustrations © Hodder Education
Typeset in Folio 10/12pt by DC Graphic Design Limited, Swanley Village, Kent
Printed in Spain

A catalogue record for this title is available from the British Library

ISBN 978 1444 189 261

Contents

1: Cells

You will revise:
- similarities and differences between plant cells and animal cells
- basic parts of cells and their function
- scientific methods of studying cells.
- the difference between cells, tissues, organs and systems
- the functions of some specialist cells
- how cells reproduce, enabling an organism to grow.

Get started

Cells are the building blocks of living things. However, most cells are so small you need a microscope to see them. When you look at cells from animals and plants through a microscope you can see their similarities and their differences.

Different cells carry out different functions. One reason for this is that cells can have very different shapes. An amazing function of cells is their ability to create new ones. This allows organisms to reproduce and grow.

Practice

1 Why did we not know about cells until the seventeenth century?

2 Write down three things that might be in plant cells but are never in animal cells.

3 Write down three things that are in both plant and animal cells.

4 Many cells specialise in absorbing material from their surroundings. What is important about the shape of these cells?

5 What are cilia? What do they do?

6 Why are nerve cells sometimes very long?

Challenge

7 **a** Here is a diagram of a simple cell. Label all of the parts.

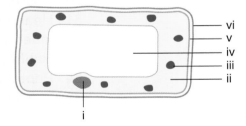

b Is this an animal cell or a plant cell?

8 Copy and complete this table.

Part of cell	Function
a	Controls what the cell actually does
Cell membrane	b
c	Place where all the chemical reactions happen
Cell wall	d

9 The largest known cell is about the same size as a small melon. What type of cell do you think this is?

10 Why do plant cells need cell walls but animal cells don't?

11 How does a plant use the vacuoles in its cells to keep it upright?

12 Explain why using a stain can help you to study the structure of cells under a microscope.

13 The diagrams below show two different cells from the same plant.

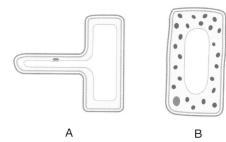

A   B

 a Where would you find these cells on a plant?

 b Explain why cell A has no chloroplasts but cell B has lots of chloroplasts.

 c Why does cell A have an elongated shape?

 d Another specialised plant cell is pollen. Why does a pollen cell have a very tough outer layer?

14 The diagrams below show three different cells found in humans.

A B C

 a Which one of these cells is present in all humans?

 b What is special about the shape of cell B that allows it to carry out its function?

 c Why does cell A have a tail?
  Why does cell C have a very large amount of cytoplasm?

15 Here is a sequence of diagrams showing how organisms grow by forming new cells. Unfortunately they have been jumbled up. Write down the correct order.

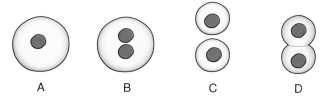

A   B   C   D

16 The longest cells known are over 1 m long. What sort of cells are these? Why can you only see them if you use a microscope?

17 Does a virus have a cell structure?

How did I do?

I can write down the basic parts of animal cells and plant cells.	✔
I can explain what these basic parts do.	☐
I can do simple calculations involving magnification.	☐
I can identify key variables in an investigation and decide which of these need to be controlled.	☐
I understand the difference between cells, tissues, organs and systems.	☐
I can recognise the shape and structure of epithelial cells, root hair, pollen, neurones, sperm, eggs, red blood cells.	☐
I can describe the function of these cells.	☐
I can explain how cells divide and how genetic information gets 'passed on' to offspring.	☐

Teacher's tips

It is vital that you know the names of the **structures** found in animal and plant cells as well as the **functions** of these parts. The only way to achieve this is to sit down and learn them. You should also be able to recognise these structures on diagrams of animal and plant cells.

2: Reproduction

You will revise:
- how reproduction takes place at a cellular level
- different strategies that species have developed for successful reproduction
- how these strategies affect the chances of survival for the young
- the main features of the human reproductive system.

Get started

The ability to reproduce successfully is essential for a species to survive. Plants and animals have developed different strategies for reproduction but there are similarities.

Practice

1. What are sex cells?

2. Identify the male and female sex cells of **a** plants and **b** animals.

3. Why does external fertilisation need many more eggs for successful reproduction?

4. Explain why mammals tend to produce fewer young than non-mammals.

Challenge

5. This question is about the similarities and differences between reproduction in plants and animals.

   a. In terms of male and female sex cells, what is the main similarity between the reproduction of plants and animals? How does this differ from single-celled creatures such as the amoeba?

   b. Some flowers can self-pollinate. What does this mean? Why can't a similar process happen in animals?

   c. Why do plants try to disperse their seeds as far away as possible? Explain how this is very different to the behaviour of many animals.

6. A female cod lays about 6 million eggs in one go. These eggs are fertilised externally and float to the top of the sea.

   a. Explain how the male cod fertilises the eggs externally.

   b. Give two reasons why many of these eggs don't grow into young cod. For each reason suggest a method that other species have developed to ensure a greater survival rate.

   c. Some fish look after their eggs in their mouths. Explain why this strategy means that the fish don't have to produce so many eggs in the first place.

d The vast majority of the young cod do not become old enough to reproduce for themselves. What are the two main factors that affect the number of sexually mature adult cod?

e Although the cod's method of reproduction is quite wasteful, what is its main advantage?

7 Here is a diagram of the human female reproductive system.

   a Label the parts and explain their functions.

   b Why is it called a system?

   c On the diagram, identify i a tissue and ii an organ.

   d Where does fertilisation of the egg take place?

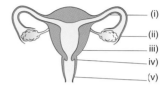

   e In terms of fertilisation, explain the difference between the formation of identical and non-identical twins.

   f Explain the role of mammary glands in increasing the chances of survival for the young.

8 An early attempt to explain how humans can reproduce is the homunculus theory. This stated that there was a little person contained in the sperm of the father. This little person grew larger in the mother's womb until it became a baby. Although this theory could explain many of the facts there were a few problems with it.

   a Why could the homunculus theory not explain all of a child's inherited characteristics?

   b The theory stated that a baby boy would also contain sperm. In the sperm would be miniature people as well – just like in the sperm of the original father. Explain how this leads to a major flaw in the theory.

9 Explain the difference between something that is hereditary and something that is inherited.

10 What are mitochondria? Why do sperm cells have a large number of them?

11 What is the main difference in the way that bacteria and viruses reproduce?

12 Explain the major benefit of sexual reproduction compared to asexual reproduction.

How did I do?

✔

I can describe the similarities and differences between plant and animal reproduction. ☐

I can discuss the advantages and disadvantages of internal fertilisation compared to external fertilisation. ☐

I can outline the main parts of the human reproductive system. ☐

Teacher's tips

Make sure you appreciate that it is **sexual reproduction** that gives rise to the immense **variety** we see around us in the animal and plant kingdoms, and **asexual reproduction** that maintains the **status quo** between generations.

3: Habitats, food chains and food webs

Get started

Organisms have evolved to live in an extremely wide variety of habitats. Not only have they adapted to everyday conditions but they have developed strategies to cope with both daily and seasonal changes.

All organisms need energy to survive. By feeding, energy from the producers can work its way up the food chain. Food webs help us to study how different species interact with each other.

Practice

1 What essential resources do plants and animals need from their habitat?

2 In any one particular habitat, why do you find different animals at different times of day?

3 State and explain two advantages of animals producing their young in the spring.

4 Why do some animals need very large habitats in order to survive?

5 What is meant by a producers, b primary consumers, c secondary consumers?

6 Explain why a primary consumer can't be a carnivore.

7 Describe the difference between a food chain and a food web.

8 What do the arrows represent in food chains and food webs?

Challenge

9 Plants and animals have adopted strategies to avoid climatic stress due to the changing seasons.

a What is meant by *climatic stress*?

b State two factors that reduce the chances of survival in the winter.

c Give an example of i an animal that hibernates and ii an animal that migrates. Explain the advantages and disadvantages of each of these two actions.

d Some animals grow a thick, white coat in preparation for the winter. Suggest two reasons why they do this.

e Explain the term *dormancy* and how this is related to the overwintering of deciduous trees.

f Why do plants in woods often grow and flower in very early spring?

10 Sometimes at the seaside you can see a marked line where the type of plants that are growing suddenly changes.

    a What is the cause of this line?

    b The habitat below the line is damper and more salty. How could you test whether it is the dampness or the salinity that the plants prefer?

11 This question is about the adaptation of animals that are predators or prey. Explain why the following are useful.

    a Nocturnal pit vipers have infrared sensors below their eyes.

    b A lion has sharp teeth and claws.

    c A deer has eyes on the side of its head.

    d A fox has eyes on the front its head.

    e Both predators and prey are sometimes camouflaged.

    f Some insects have black and yellow stripes.

    g Hunted animals live in big groups.

12 Here is a diagram of a food web from a woodland habitat.

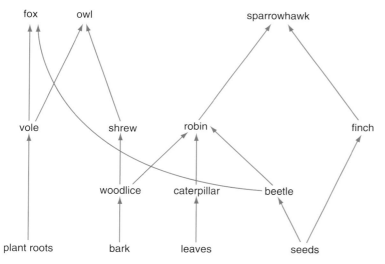

    a Draw all of the possible food chains from this food web.

    b If the numbers of beetles diminished, what would happen to the population of robins?

    c Although there will be more seeds, why might the number of finches decrease if the number of beetles decreases?

Teacher's tips

One of the best ways to appreciate the **adaptations** an organism shows due to its environment is to **imagine** you are that organism and ask yourself what characteristics would allow you to be successful.

4: Variation

You will revise:

- characteristics that are inherited or due to the environment
- how the origin of different characteristics can be investigated
- the difficulty in studying characteristics in humans and how this can be overcome.

Get started

Members within a species can vary quite differently from each other. Sometimes the cause of this variation is hereditary; sometimes the cause is environmental – but often the cause is due to both factors.

Practice

1. What is meant by an *inherited characteristic*?

2. Explain how the height of trees can vary due to environmental conditions.

3. Why, on the whole, is the variation between different species much more than the variation within one species?

Challenge

4. Although humans share many similarities there are also many differences between them. For each statement, decide whether the characteristic is *inherited* or *due to the environment* or *both*. Give a reason for each answer.

   A Gender
   B Language they speak
   C Confidence
   D Pattern of fingerprint
   E Score on a maths test
   F Eye colour
   G Height
   H Number of limbs
   I Ability to learn to speak
   J Natural shape of nose
   K Table manners

5. A pupil wanted to investigate whether the environment affects the height of candytuft flowers. She planted some seeds and grew them in different parts of the garden. She noticed that the candytuft did indeed grow to different heights.

   a Apart from environmental factors, what other variable might be responsible for the different heights?

   The pupil decided to repeat the experiment. However, this time she grew all of the candytuft from cuttings taken from a single plant.

   b How could she be sure that this time she was carrying out a fair test?

6 A pupil investigated whether there is a relationship between height and weight for pupils in her school. She measured five pupils from a Year 7 class and five pupils from a Year 11 class. Here is the data that she obtained.

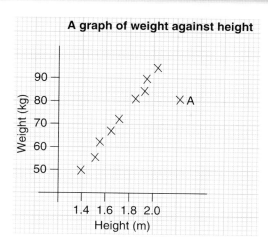

a Are height and weight continuous or discontinuous variables? Explain your answer.

b The graph shows that there is a positive correlation between height and weight. What does *positive correlation* mean?

c Why are there two distinct areas on the graph?

d The pupil stated that 'the taller you are, the heavier you are'. Is this strictly true?

e Suggest what the person who produced point A would look like.

f Give two reasons why this person might be like this.

7 **a** Most twins are brought up in exactly the same environment. What must be the major cause of variation between non-identical twins?

b Some identical twins have been separated at birth and brought up in entirely different environments. Why is this useful for scientists studying how different factors lead to variation?

8 Is the gender of alligators due to inheritance or the environment?

9 What are feral children? How do they help us to understand the environmental causes of variation?

10 Explain why the variation between domesticated animals (such as dogs and sheep) seems to group them into breeds compared to the more random variation of wild animals.

How did I do?

I can describe how variation can be due to inheritance, to the environment, or to both.	✔ ☐
I can discuss various human characteristics and distinguish whether they are hereditary or environmental.	☐
I understand what is meant by a fair test.	☐
I understand the use of identical twins and feral children in the study of variation.	☐

Teacher's tips

Remember that **continuous data** is plotted on a **line graph** and **discontinuous data** on a **bar chart** or **pie chart**.

5: Classifying living things

You will revise:
- the use of a key to identify a species
- how animals are classified into vertebrates and invertebrates
- the five main classes of vertebrates
- how the classification system has evolved.

Get started

Scientists try to organise different species into a system of groups based on their similarities. This makes different organisms much easier to study and identify. However, it can sometimes be very difficult to fit a particular organism into the system.

Practice

1. Explain the purpose of a key.

2. What are the two main kingdoms?

3. How is the animal kingdom divided up first?

Challenge

4. All animals and plants are given a name in Latin. This name has two parts: the first part is called the genus (a group of similar animals) and the second part is the species. So the lion is called *Panthera leo* since it is part of the big cat (*Panthera*) genus and the lion species is called *leo*.

   a. What defines a species?

   b. Why are the names in Latin?

   c. Lions are also mammals (mammalia). If you wanted to extend the name *Panthera leo* to include this bit of information, where would you write mammalia? Explain your answer.

5. Here is a diagram of the main groups of the animal kingdom. Copy the diagram and add the missing words.

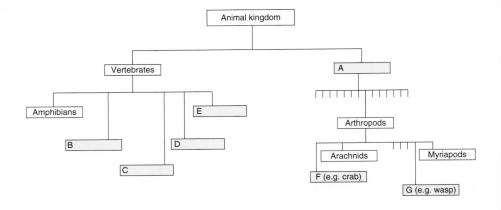

6　**a**　What features of a housefly class it as an insect?

　　b　What features of a housefly class it as an arthropod?

　　c　What feature of a housefly classes it as an invertebrate?

　　d　State one feature of a housefly that classes it as an animal (rather than a plant).

7　There are five classes of vertebrates. For each class write one or two features that are specific only to that class.

8　**a**　Suggest why, following discoveries of new organisms, there were only two kingdoms to start with, but there are now five.

　　b　The duck-billed platypus lays eggs. However, it has hair on its body and produces milk. Explain why this poses a problem for its classification.

9　The full classification of a lion actually uses seven ranks: kingdom, phylum, class, order, family, genus and species. Question 1 gives the Latin words for the class, genus and species of the lion. What are the Latin names for the other four ranks that the lion belongs to?

10　You can actually split the ranks up further into kingdom, phylum, subphylum, superdivision, division, superclass, class, subclass, order, superfamily, family, subfamily, genus, species and subspecies!

　　a　Why did scientists need more and more levels as their knowledge increased?

　　b　Find the 15 ranks that humans belong to.

11　Although the duck-billed platypus poses a problem for its classification, why has it been classed as a mammal?

12　Some scientists are trying to classify organisms into evolutionary groups – a little bit like a family tree. In this system, humans are closely related to chimps because we share a common ancestor. How is this different to the current way of classifying things? Why wasn't this done in the first place?

How did I do?

I can use a key to identify a species.	✔ ☐
I can distinguish between vertebrates and invertebrates.	☐
I can write about the five main species of vertebrate.	☐
I understand why the classification system has evolved over time.	☐

Teacher's tips

In order to help you remember the seven ranks used in the classification of organisms, make up a **mnemonic** using the first letter of each rank – K,P,C,O,F,G,S to help you remember the order.

6: Acids and alkalis

You will revise:

▶ the harmful effects of acids and alkalis

▶ how to handle strong acids and alkalis carefully

▶ acids and alkalis used in everyday solutions.

▶ the pH scale

▶ using indicators to determine the pH

▶ how a universal indicator works

▶ neutralisation of acids and alkalis.

Get started

Solutions of chemicals are acidic, alkaline or neutral. Strong acids and alkalis are dangerous and need handling with care. However, weaker acids and alkalis are used in everyday items.

Indicators are materials that change colour when an acid or an alkali is applied to them. Universal indicators can be used to find the pH of a substance. The pH value indicates how acidic or alkaline a substance is.

Practice

1 Explain the meanings of the words *corrosive* and *caustic*.

2 What is the difference between a base and an alkali?

3 What colour does litmus paper turn when it is put in an acid? What colour does it turn in an alkali?

4 What is the pH of pure water?

5 Explain why a universal indicator can be used to find a pH value, but litmus paper can't.

Challenge

6 Here is a diagram of three warning signs found on the packaging of some chemicals.

    A   B   C

a State what each warning sign means.

b Suggest two safety precautions you need to take when handling chemicals that are corrosive.

c Why do you need to be particularly careful when dealing with harmful gases?

d Why is it important to display hazard warning symbols clearly on lorries carrying dangerous chemicals?

7 You can dilute acids with water. You need to be careful with sulfuric acid. The acid's reaction with water produces a lot of heat. It is safer to add the acid to the water rather than the other way round.

    a Why is it dangerous to add water to sulfuric acid?

    b Explain why it is safer to add the acid to the water instead.

8 A wasp sting has a pH of 10 and a bee sting has a pH of 2.

    a Which sting is an acid and which is an alkali?

    b What colour would each sting turn some universal indicator paper?

    c If you mixed some bee sting and some wasp sting together, within what pH range must the resulting mixture lie?

    d Write some instructions telling someone what they can do to neutralise wasp and bee stings using common household products.

9 This table shows the colour of some indicators at different pH values.

Indicator	pH value													
	1	2	3	4	5	6	7	8	9	10	11	12	13	14
A	Colourless							Blue						Red
B	Red				Yellow			Green				Blue		
C	Colourless			Yellow			Green			Blue			Red	

    a What is the colour of each indicator when a neutral substance is added?

    b Indicator B is currently green in colour. What colour changes would it go through if you gradually added more and more sulfuric acid?

    c All of the indicators were mixed together. Assuming that the indicators carried on behaving in the same way, write down the colour of the mixture at the following pH values:

      i 1   **ii** 4.5   **iii** 6   **iv** 12   **v** 14

    d Why is it useful to mix different indicator dyes together?

How did I do?

I can describe the harmful effects of acids and alkalis.	✔ ☐
I can write instructions on how to handle strong acids and alkalis carefully and safely.	☐
I can recognise standard warning signs used to label dangerous chemicals.	☐
I can list some common acids and alkalis used in household products.	☐
I can outline the pH scale and typical values for weak and strong acids and alkalis.	☐
I can draw a chart to represent the colour a universal indicator turns for different pH values.	☐
I can give an example of a neutral solution and its pH.	☐
I can explain the process of neutralisation.	☐

Teacher's tips

The pH scale runs from1 to 14. pH values 1 to 6 are acidic and pH values 8 to 14 are alkali. You need to appreciate that the further away from pH7 the stronger the acid or alkali is. So an acid with a pH of 1 is a stronger acid than an acid with a pH of 3.

7: Chemical reactions and burning

You will revise:

- standard tests for hydrogen and carbon dioxide
- the difference between physical processes and chemical reactions
- chemical reactions involving metals and carbonates with acids
- representing chemical reactions with word equations.
- the chemical reactions that happen when materials burn
- word equations to represent these reactions
- experimental evidence that burning involves a chemical reaction with oxygen.

Get started

Sometimes, when you put a metal or a carbonate in acid, you get bubbles of gas. You can collect the gas to test what type it is. The gas is a new substance that has been formed from the chemical reaction.

When a fuel burns it is reacting with oxygen. Heat energy starts the reaction, but once the reaction is underway a lot of heat is released.

Practice

1 What is the difference between a chemical change and a physical change?

2 State the terms used for **a** the chemicals that are present before a reaction takes place and **b** the new chemicals that have been produced by the reaction.

3 What is the scientific name for burning?

4 Why do objects burn more vigorously in pure oxygen rather than air?

5 Explain the difference between burning and exploding.

Challenge

6 **a** What two elements must be present in a carbonate?

   b Therefore, what does the *ate* stand for in a word equation?

   c Where does the word *hydrated* come from?

7 Why does limewater go milky?

8 Some magnesium was burnt in oxygen. Write a word equation for the chemical reaction taking place.

9 How does a fire blanket put out a kitchen fire?

10 Methane gas contains both carbon and hydrogen. When methane burns, both the carbon and hydrogen react with the oxygen in the air.

   a Copy and complete the word equation for this process:

   methane + ... → . . . . . . + ... dioxide

   b Methane is a fossil fuel. What product of the reaction is a problem for the environment? Explain your answer.

11 An experiment was set up to investigate the burning of a candle using this apparatus.

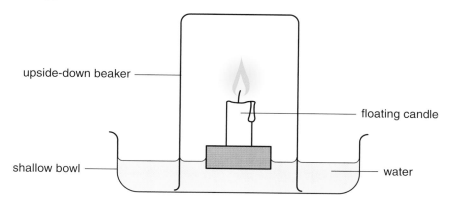

upside-down beaker

floating candle

shallow bowl

water

a Why did the candle eventually go out?

b Explain why the water went up inside the beaker.

c How would the results differ if the air in the beaker was replaced by the gases collected by pupils blowing into balloons?

How did I do?

I understand the meaning of reactants, products and chemical reactions. ✔

I can describe the standard tests for hydrogen and carbon dioxide. ☐

I can write word equations for the reactions between metals and carbonates in acids. ☐

I can write a word equation for the chemical reaction that is happening when an element burns. ☐

I can explain and analyse the results of the burning candle experiment. ☐

I can describe the standard test for oxygen. ☐

Teacher's tips

All chemical reactions involve the formation of one or more new substances. When you are writing a word equation, to summarise a chemical equation, remember to put the **reactants** on the **left** hand side of the arrow and the **products** on the **right**. List each reactant and each product separately.

8: The particle model of matter

You will revise:
- the main features of solids, liquids and gases
- how these can be explained using the particle model
- what happens when materials change state.

Get started

The idea that matter is composed of very tiny particles helps to explain lots of physical phenomena. The particle model can be used to explain the three states of matter: solids, liquids and gases.

Practice

1. The particle model seems obvious today. Why were scientists sceptical about it in the past?

2. A material that can flow is called a *fluid*. Which states of matter are fluids?

3. Draw diagrams to demonstrate how the particles are arranged in solids, liquids and gases.

Challenge

4. Copy and complete this table summarising the physical properties of solids, liquids and gases.

State of matter	Shape	Volume	Ability to flow	Compressibility
Solid	a	Stays fixed	b	Can't really be compressed
Liquid	c	d	e	f
Gas	Becomes shape of container	g	h	i

5. In terms of the particle model of matter explain the following:

   a Solids have a fixed shape and size.

   b Liquids have a fixed size but not a fixed shape.

   c Gases have neither a fixed shape nor size.

   d Gases can be compressed easily but liquids and solids can't.

   e A given mass of gas takes up more volume than the same mass of a solid.

   f Increasing the pressure on a gas can turn it into a liquid.

6 One major difference between the states of matter is in the motion of the particles. For each of the three states of matter, describe the way in which the particles move.

7 a Suggest two reasons why gold is heavier than the same volume of copper.

b Suggest one reason why water is heavier than the same volume of steam.

c Materials expand when they get hotter. What happens to the size of the particles?

8 a Give an example of a material that freezes at a very high temperature.

b Give an example of a material that boils at a very low temperature.

c Why do you need energy to make something melt or boil?

9 Copy and complete this table about the changes of state.

State change	Name	Temperature at which water changes state	Bonds made or broken?	Energy needed or energy given out?
Solid to liquid	a	b	c	Needed
Liquid to gas	Boiling	d	Broken	e
Gas to liquid	f	100 °C	g	h
Liquid to solid	i	j	Made	Given out

10 Do the particles ever stop moving? If so, at what temperature do they do this?

11 There is a fourth state of matter. What is this called? How can it be explained using a particle theory?

12 What are the similarities and differences between boiling and evaporation?

13 Graphite and diamond are two different forms of solid carbon. Graphite is very soft but diamond is very hard. How can the particle model explain why they are so different?

How did I do?

	✔
I can write a sentence stating the particle model of matter.	☐
I know the main features of solids, liquids and gases.	☐
I can explain these features using the particle model.	☐
I can describe what happens when matter changes state.	☐

Teacher's tips

If you want to impress someone with your deeper knowledge, there's an additional state change you should be aware of. It's called **sublimation** and involves a change in state from a solid directly into a gas or vice versa.

9: Solutions

You will revise:

- the meaning of solvent, solute and solution
- how forming solutions can be explained using the particle model
- solubility, and how this changes with temperature
- using the conservation of mass to study physical and chemical processes.
- how filtration separates out undissolved material
- the process of distillation for collecting a solvent
- separating mixtures of solutions using chromatography.

Get started

When salt dissolves in water it seems to disappear. The particle model of matter can be used to explain what really happens.

Solutions are mixtures of solutes and solvents. These are physical rather than chemical mixtures so it is fairly easy to separate them again. You need to know several techniques.

Practice

1. What is the difference between a solute, a solvent and a solution?

2. When something dissolves, is a chemical reaction happening?

3. Why can't you filter out a solute from a solvent?

4. What is meant by evaporation and condensation?

5. Why does distilling an alcoholic drink make it more alcoholic?

Challenge

6. What is meant by the conservation of mass? How can it be applied to solutes, solvents and solutions?

7. a What is a saturated solution? Use the particle model of matter to explain how solutions can become saturated.

   b Define solubility.

   c The solubility of potassium nitrate in water is 35 g per 100 g of water at room temperature. What is the maximum mass of potassium nitrate you can dissolve in 150 g of water?

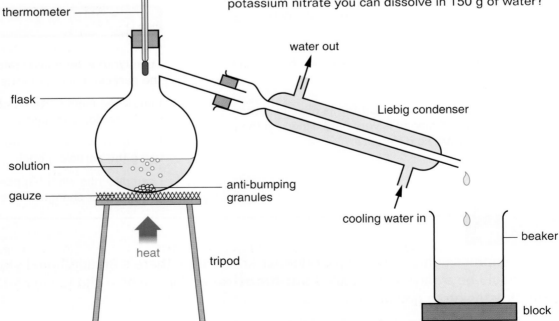

8 The diagram shows some apparatus used for separating solutions.

   a What is this method called?

   b Which part of the solution would you collect from this process?

   c Explain in terms of particles how this process works.

9 Here is a list of instructions to follow to obtain pure salt from rock salt (a mixture of pure salt and grit).

A Dissolve the rock salt in water.
B Filter the mixture and collect the filtrate.
C Evaporate the filtrate in a warm oven.

   a In terms of particles, explain as fully as you can how the pure salt is separated from the rock salt.

   b Why is the procedure a little more effective if you use warm water to dissolve the rock salt rather than cold water?

   c Suggest what you could do to the rock salt before you dissolved it to make the procedure more effective.

   d What calculation would you make to find the percentage of pure salt in the original rock salt sample?

   e If the whole class did this experiment (from the same source of rock salt), how could you find out whose procedure was the most effective?

10 A forensic scientist wanted to check the composition of some ink. She made a chromatogram comparing the ink with some known dyes.

   a Which dyes (A, B, C, D) are present in the ink? Explain your answer.

   b In terms of the particles of solutes, explain how chromatography works.

11 What is fractional distillation? What is it used for?

ink   A B C D

How did I do?

I can use the particle model to describe what happens when a solute dissolves in a solvent. ✔

I can explain why some materials dissolve but not others. ☐

I can determine solubility at a given temperature from a graph. ☐

I understand and can use the principle of conservation of mass. ☐

I can describe how filtration works using the particle model. ☐

I can outline the basic stages of separating pure salt from rock salt. ☐

I can explain how distillation can be used to collect a solvent. ☐

I can deduce what dyes are present in ink by using a chromatogram. ☐

Teacher's tips

If you are asked to show how the term '**conservation of mass**' can be demonstrated with respect to solutions – it's easy. Take a beaker and add 150g of water. Dissolve 25g of sugar in the water and reweigh. The total mass will be 175g – the sum of the water (the solvent) and sugar (the solute).

10: Energy transfer

Get started

Whenever we do something, energy is transferred. So when a fuel burns, energy is transferred from the fuel as heat and light. A good energy resource allows us to transfer energy from it easily in useful ways.

Once energy has passed from the Sun up the food chain, it can be used by fungi and bacteria when organisms decompose to set up further food chains. Fossil fuels are used by humans to provide electrical energy and warmth for our homes. It is finally released in the form of heat into space, never to be used again.

Practice

1 Why are fossil fuels running out?

2 Explain the difference between renewable and non-renewable resources.

3 What do we call the energy resource obtained from living things?

4 Write down the two units that we use to state the energy content of foods.

Challenge

5 This question is about fossil fuels.

   a In what form is energy stored in fossil fuels? Where does this energy originally come from?

   b Explain why you can obtain much more energy from 1 kg of coal than you can from 1 kg of wood.

   c We burn fossil fuels in power stations to produce electricity. Why is electricity called a secondary fuel?

   d State two uses of fossil fuels other than for heating or producing electricity.

   e State two advantages and two disadvantages of using fossil fuels to produce electricity.

6 Solar panels and solar cookers are two examples of using energy from the Sun directly. Solar panels use energy from the Sun to produce electricity. Solar cookers focus the Sun's rays to a point where food can be cooked.

   a What is meant by *using the energy from the Sun directly*?

   b Explain why solar panels are black but solar cookers are silver.

   c Suggest why solar panels have a very large surface area.

   d What is the main problem of using these devices in the UK?

   e Both solar panels and solar cookers tend to be used the most in remote areas. Suggest a reason for this.

7 What arrangement of the Sun, Earth and Moon gives the most tidal energy?

8 **a** Only about 10% of the energy gets passed from one organism to another up the food chain. Where does the rest of the energy end up?

    b Suggest why it is much easier for organisms to obtain energy from food than it is for them to use heat energy from their surroundings.

9 A chocolate ice-cream bar contains 700 000 joules of energy.

    a If it takes 700 J of energy to lift a man up by 1 m, then how high could a man climb up a mountain using the energy of just one ice-cream bar?

    b Explain why your answer to **a** is likely to be a huge overestimate.

10 The diagram shows some apparatus you can use to compare the energy contained in different foods.

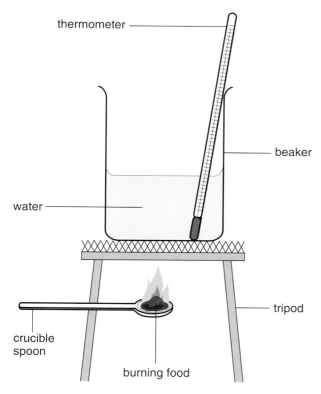

thermometer

beaker

water

tripod

crucible spoon

burning food

    a State the independent and the dependent variables.

    b Identify three key control variables and how you can keep them constant.

    c Why is it important that you keep control variables constant?

    d What sort of graph should you plot to summarise the results?

    e By referring to question **5c**, how could you calculate the actual amount of energy stored in the food?

    f Why would your calculation be an underestimate?

11 Why is glucose an important source of energy for humans?

12 How does the human body store energy from its food?

Teacher's tips

The data given for energy content on food packets are obtained using apparatus that does not allow heat loss during burning. The value you would obtain doing the experiment shown here, to compare the energy content in different foods, will be lower for several reasons. It's worth thinking about these so that you could list them in an examination. A few of the reasons are:

- not all of the food is burnt
- some heat is lost to the air
- some heat is transferred to the glass beaker and mounted needle and not all to the water.

11: Electric current

You will revise:
- the main features of a series circuit
- how the number of cells and the resistance affect the size of the current
- where energy is transformed in a circuit
- simple parallel circuits.

Get started

An electric current flows when a cell is connected to a complete circuit. In a series circuit, the current is the same at all points. However, energy can be transferred out in other forms: as heat (in a heater) or light (by a bulb) or sound (in a bell).

Practice

1 Describe the difference between series and parallel circuits.

2 What is electrical resistance?

3 Name the device you use to measure electrical current.

4 What is the unit of electric current?

5 Explain the difference between a battery and a cell.

Challenge

6 This question is about designing a circuit to make a torch.

   a Here is a drawing of a light bulb. Copy the diagram and label where you would connect the wires.

   b Add the rest of the circuit to your drawing. Include a cell and a switch.

   c In what direction does the current go?

   d Does it matter where you put the switch in a series circuit? Explain your answer.

   e What could you do in order to make the light bulb brighter?

   f Light bulbs emit light in all directions. Name two features of a torch that result in the light being emitted in a fairly straight beam.

7 Here are four series circuits A–D with identical cells and light bulbs.

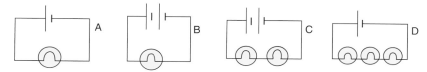

   a Write down the circuit:

    i that has the most resistance

    ii that has the highest current

    iii where the cells run down the quickest

    iv that has the dimmest bulbs

    v where the current is used up the most.

   b In which two circuits will the brightness of the bulbs be the same as each other?

   c Explain, in as much detail as you can, what happens to the energy in circuit D.

8 Write down what ammeters A_1, A_2 and A_3 would read on these two circuits. Assume that all the light bulbs are identical. The readings on two other ammeters have been written in already.

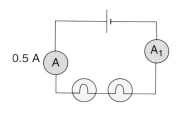 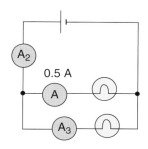

9 Explain why it is much harder to locate a broken bulb in a set of Christmas tree lights connected in series than in parallel.

Teacher's tips

If you are finding electric currents difficult to visualise then try to liken the flow of charge around a circuit to the flow of water through a system of pipes. A **pump** drives the **water** round the **pipes** in the same way that a **cell** pushes the **charge** around a **circuit**. Water is not used up during its passage through the pipes and neither is the electric current used up as it flows around a circuit.

12: Forces and stretching

You will revise:

- the definition of a force and its unit
- how we measure forces
- different types of force
- how springs and elastic bands stretch differently.
- the difference between mass and weight
- using density to determine whether something floats or sinks
- the forces involved in floating and sinking.

 Get started

A force is a push or a pull. Pulling springs and elastic bands at both ends makes them stretch but they behave differently. A very common force is friction, which can sometimes be useful and sometimes be a nuisance.

Although the words *mass* and *weight* are interchangeable in everyday life, they mean very different things in science. When objects are in fluids, the weight and the upthrust combine to produce a resultant force which can make them float or sink. You can also consider floating and sinking in terms of density.

 Practice

1. Define what we mean by a force,

2. What is the unit of force?

3. How can you measure the size of a force?

4. Which quantity is a force: mass or weight?

5. When an object is floating, what is the relationship between the upthrust and the object's weight?

 Challenge

6. You have been asked to produce a graph showing how the extension of an elastic band depends on the force stretching it.

   a. State two safety precautions you would need to take while carrying out the measurements.

   b. Suggest a procedure for measuring the extension of the elastic band.

   c. Why do you need to take repeat readings?

   d. When you draw the graph you might spot an anomalous point. What is an anomalous point? How would you recognise it?

   e. Here is the shape of the graph you obtained (without the anomalous point). Copy the shape of the graph and label the regions where the elastic band is stiff. Explain your answer.

   f. Why is it better to use springs rather than elastic bands in forcemeters?

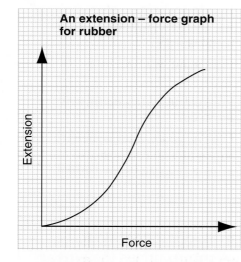

An extension – force graph for rubber

Extension

Force

7 Draw a picture of a book on a table. Use arrows to indicate the forces acting on the book. Remember that the length of an arrow represents the size of the force.

8 State two ways in which friction is useful for riding a bicycle and two ways in which it is a nuisance. Explain what measures you can take to reduce the effect of friction when it is a nuisance.

9 Explain why you can slide much further on ice skates than you can in flat shoes when you are on an ice rink.

10 This question is about mass and weight.

   a Explain what is meant by the mass and the weight of an object. State the unit for each of these quantities.

   b How do your mass and your weight change when you go into space?

   c You can find your mass using normal bathroom scales. Would these work on the Moon?

   d If the Earth pulls with a force of 10 N per kg of matter, what would be the weight of a 2 kg object?

   e What would be the mass of this 2 kg object if it went to the planet Jupiter?

11 An object is hanging from a forcemeter. The meter reads a force of 2 N.

   a Why does the reading on the forcemeter decrease when the object is lowered into some water?

   b Once the object is totally immersed the meter reads 0.5 N. What is the size of the upthrust?

   c Another object of the same volume has a weight of 1 N. Explain what happens when this object is lowered into the water.

How did I do?

	✔
I can describe what we mean by a force and how we measure its size.	☐
I can distinguish between contact and non-contact forces.	☐
I can explain the difference between springs and elastic bands when they are stretched.	☐
I can examine the different roles of friction when someone is riding a bicycle.	☐
I can state what we mean by mass and weight.	☐
I can calculate the density of an object.	☐
I can describe the forces acting on a hot-air balloon when it is rising up.	☐

Teacher's tips

Examination papers often involve **graphical interpretation**. This topic lends itself to this task. The easiest way to describe the shape of a graph is to divide it up into a number of sections and then describe each section separately. In order to score maximum marks make sure that you include reference to the values on the **x and y axis** to make it absolutely clear to the examiner which part of the graph you are referring to.

13: The Solar System

You will revise:

- the motion of the Earth as it orbits the Sun
- how this motion leads to the seasons
- why we see different phases of the Moon.
- the structure of the Solar System and the objects within it
- different ways of observing the Universe
- searching for extra-terrestrial life.

Get started

The way in which the Earth moves through space gives rise to many phenomena. These include day and night, the seasons and both solar and lunar eclipses.

Practice

1. Explain why countries at different longitudes have different time zones.

2. What is the difference between a solar and a lunar eclipse?

3. Describe the apparent motion of the stars during the night (in the northern hemisphere) and explain the cause of this motion.

4. Which of the following are luminous sources and which simply reflect light: stars, planets, comets, the Moon?

5. Name the planets in the correct order, starting from the one nearest the Sun.

6. What is the brightest planet in the night sky? Why is it the brightest?

7. What is the Solar System? What objects are in it?

Challenge

8. This question is about the phases of the Moon.

   a For each part of the diagram below, draw the shape of the Moon as seen from Earth.

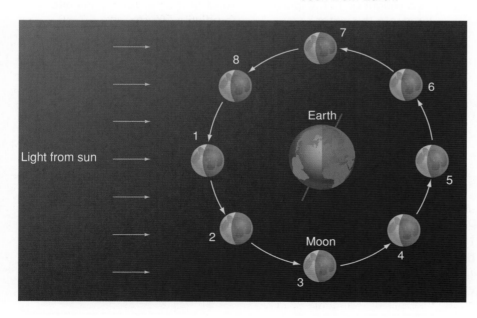

   b Sometimes the dark parts of the Moon are actually dimly lit. What is the cause of this?

9. a In the northern hemisphere, in which direction will the Sun be at midday?

   b Why does the height of the Sun at midday change throughout the year?

   c What do we call the two days where the Sun is the highest and the lowest?

d   Something else special happens on these days. What is it?

e   Explain why full sunlight is a lot hotter when the Sun is high in the sky compared to when the Sun is low in the sky.

10   Here is a diagram of the Earth and the sunlight shining on it. Copy the diagram and answer the following questions.

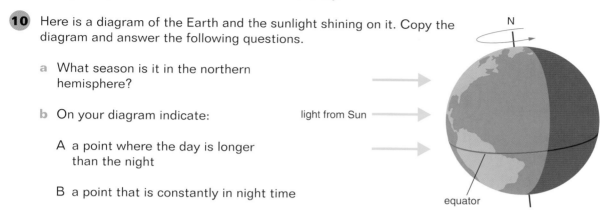

a   What season is it in the northern hemisphere?

b   On your diagram indicate:

A   a point where the day is longer than the night

B   a point that is constantly in night time

C   a point where the lengths of the day and the night are the same.

c   Why does the temperature tend to increase for about two months after the longest day?

11   a   What force is responsible for making objects orbit other objects?

b   State the difference between the orbits of planets and satellites.

c   The period of orbit (a planet's 'year') gets longer the further the planet is from the Sun. Suggest two reasons why.

d   Where do most of the asteroids orbit the Sun?

e   What do we call an asteroid that crashes onto the Earth's surface?

f   Why does the Moon's surface show many impact craters but Earth's surface doesn't?

12   SETI (the Search for Extra-Terrestrial Intelligence) uses radio receivers to pick up the presence of intelligent life forms.

a   Why will SETI only be able to detect the presence of intelligent life forms using this method?

b   There are lots of natural radio signals produced by objects in space. How would SETI be able to distinguish a signal that had been produced by intelligent life?

c   Why would it not be possible to have a long-distance conversation with extra-terrestrial life forms? (Assume they speak English!)

13   a   By observing the night sky over several days, how can you distinguish between a planet and a star?

b   What is a constellation? Why do their shapes change gradually over thousands of years?

c   State two reasons why one star seems brighter than another star.

How did I do?

I can draw a diagram of the Earth and the Sun when the northern hemisphere is in summertime.	✔
I can explain the different phases of the Moon.	
I can describe the origin of solar and lunar eclipses.	
I can draw a diagram of the Solar System and label the objects within it.	
I can explain the role of gravity in the Solar System.	
I can state the major advances in technology that have led to humans observing more and more of the Universe.	
I can discuss the various ways in which we have searched for extra-terrestrial life.	

Teacher's tips

Questions often require knowledge of the order of the planets from the Sun. Make up a **mnemonic**, using the first letter of each of each planet, to help you remember the order.

14: Food

Get started

We need food and water to keep our bodies functioning. But to keep them functioning well, we need a balanced diet appropriate to our lifestyle. We can test different foods to determine what nutrients they provide.

Practice

1 Name the five different nutrient groups.

2 Describe the use that the body makes of each of these groups.

3 What is a balanced diet?

4 Why might different people need different diets?

Challenge

5 An essential chemical that our bodies need is water. The body can survive much longer without food than it can without water.

   a 70% of a child's body mass is water. If their total mass is 50 kg, what mass of water does the child contain?

   b Explain the role of water in the human body in:

      i temperature regulation

      ii transporting chemicals around the body.

   c Suggest why the body can last longer without food than it can without water.

6 a What elements are present in carbohydrates other than oxygen?

   b If all the different types of carbohydrates contain the same elements as each other, how are they different?

   c Fibre, starch and sugar are different types of carbohydrate. Name a food source containing each type.

   d Fibre isn't digested by the body. What is it used for?

   e What is the main use of sugars and starch in the body?

7 a Explain the difference between proteins and amino acids.

   b State two uses of proteins in the body.

c Name four types of food that are good sources of protein.

d Why must vegetarians be particularly careful about the amount of protein in their diet?

8 Copy and complete this table about the different food tests.

Substance under test	Description	Outcome if substance is present
Starch	a	Solution turns blue/black
b	Add a few drops of Benedict's solution to the food solution. Heat test tube in a water bath until the solution boils.	Solution turns orange
Protein	c	Solution turns purple
d	Add some ethanol to the food solution and mix well. Then add water to solution and shake again.	Solution turns white

9 Here is some data about two different types of food.

Type of food	Protein (per 100 g)	Carbohydrate (per 100 g)	Fat (per 100 g)
A	23.8	0.0	1.0
B	13.2	65.6	2.0

a One of these types is pasta and the other is chicken. Which is which?

b Suggest why you couldn't live on these food types alone.

c Each of these food types could make up a large proportion of a balanced diet. Give an example of someone who would use type A and an example of someone who would use type B. Explain your answer.

10 Here are some diseases caused by a lack of vitamins or minerals in the body. For each disease, write down the main symptoms of the disease and the mineral or vitamin that is deficient.

a Anaemia   b Rickets

c Beriberi   d Scurvy

How did I do?

I can list the five nutrient types and explain their role in the human body. ✔ ☐

I can describe tests for starch, sugar, protein and fat. ☐

I can suggest a balanced diet for a marathon runner and a pregnant woman. ☐

Teacher's tips

Learn the food tests thoroughly. Make sure you know the reagents used, whether heat is necessary or not and most importantly not just the final colour but the **colour change**. For example the Benedicts test for sugars sees a colour change from turquoise to orange.

15: Digestion

You will revise:
- the main parts of the human digestive system
- why we need enzymes
- the right conditions for enzymes to work effectively.

Get started

Once food has entered our bodies, we extract the nutrients we need for short-term and long-term use and excrete or egest the rest. This process is called *digestion*.

Practice

1. In terms of particles, what is the main function of digestion?

2. State three functions that are performed when humans chew their food.

3. What do we call the chemicals that speed up the process of digestion? What are they made from?

4. Why does the inside of the stomach have to be acidic?

Challenge

5. Here are three types of teeth. For each type explain how they are used to break up the food.

   a Incisors   b Canines   c Molars.

6. a Label this diagram.

   b Explain why we call the digestive system a *system*.

   c The food doesn't pass through some of the organs you have labelled. Which organs are these?

   d In terms of the food passing through the alimentary canal, what are these organs used for?

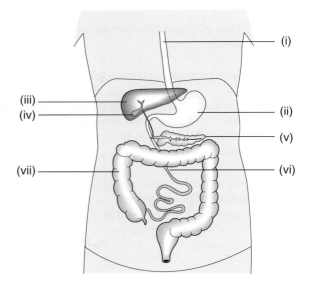

7 a Which enzyme does the stomach produce?

b How does the stomach kill bacteria?

c How does the stomach churn the food? What is the purpose of this churning?

d Why does the stomach need a thick inner wall of mucus?

8 a Why are alkaline juices added to the small intestine?

b State two functions the small intestine performs to aid digestion.

c The inner wall of the small intestine is covered with little 'finger-like' structures called *villi*. How does this help digestion?

9 a State two functions of the large intestine.

b What are the main components of faeces?

c Why do the intestines need a large blood supply?

10 Copy and complete this table.

Nutrient	Enzyme used	Where enzyme is added
Starch	a	Mouth
Protein	b	c
d	Lipase	Small intestine

11 a What is peristalsis?

b Explain why this means we can digest food upside down and in space.

12 Why does the blood supply from intestines go directly to the liver?

13 Explain the role of bile.

14 Describe the route of a glucose molecule between digestion and respiration.

How did I do?

	✔
I can label a diagram of the digestive system.	☐
I can describe the process of digestion as food passes along the alimentary canal.	☐
I can state the enzymes that digest a particular nutrient and where they are added.	☐

Teacher's tips

In order to demonstrate to yourself that the enzyme salivary amylase hydrolyses starch into maltose in the mouth take a small piece of dry bread and chew it until you can taste the sweetness of the sugar. Humans do not usually chew their food for long enough for this to happen so be prepared to chew for several minutes!

16: Blood circulation and respiration

You will revise:

- the chemical process of respiration
- why respiration is needed in the body
- how the content of exhaled air varies from inhaled air.
- how blood is used to transport chemicals around the body
- the direction of blood flow
- evidence for blood circulation.

 Get started

One important use of food is to provide us with energy. Respiration is the process in which chemical reactions in the cells release this energy so that the cells can perform all their other functions.

In order for our cells to respire, they need a supply of glucose and oxygen. Both breathing and blood circulation ensure that these resources are provided and that the waste products (carbon dioxide and water) are taken away.

 Practice

1. Write down the word equation for aerobic respiration.

2. What are the similarities between respiration and burning?

3. Which parts of the blood carry oxygen, glucose, carbon dioxide and water?

 Challenge

4. Here is a diagram showing an experiment to test the content of exhaled air.

   a. What chemical does the apparatus test for?

   b. Explain what happens when you breathe gently in and out through the middle tube.

   c. How does this show that the chemical must be more concentrated in the exhaled air?

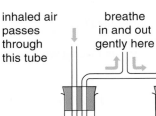

inhaled air passes through this tube

breathe in and out gently here

exhaled air passes through this tube

lime-water

5 **a** Explain why mammals tend to respire a lot more than reptiles.

  b How do we know that both oxygen and carbon dioxide must dissolve in water?

6 Explain why both blood circulation and breathing are needed for successful respiration in the cells.

7 Below is an incomplete schematic diagram of blood circulation.

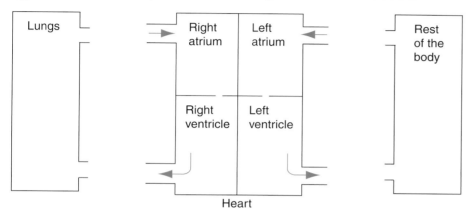

Heart

Copy and complete the diagram to show how blood circulates around the body.

8 Explain the role of haemoglobin in transporting oxygen.

9 Why is there a vein that carries oxygenated blood? What is its name?

10 What is the role of the kidneys in maintaining a healthy blood supply?

How did I do?

	✔
I can write a word equation and a balanced symbol equation for respiration.	☐
I can explain the main benefit of respiration.	☐
I can describe an experiment to show that organisms respire.	☐
I can analyse the content of inhaled and exhaled air and explain why they are different.	☐
I can describe how blood flows between the heart, the lungs and the rest of the body.	☐
I can distinguish between veins, arteries and capillaries.	☐
I can explain the role of blood circulation in the respiration of cells.	☐

Teacher's tips

The flow of blood through the heart and lungs can be remembered by VAVAVAVA.
Heart: **v**ein (vena cava) **a**trium (right) **v**entricle (right) **a**rtery (pulmonary)

Lungs: **v**ein (pulmonary) **a**trium (left) **v**entricle (left) **a**rtery (aorta).

You will revise:

▶ bacteria, viruses and fungi

▶ experimental methods for studying micro-organisms

▶ how to calculate the size of a bacteria colony.

▶ how diseases are spread

▶ the human immune system

▶ antibiotics and vaccinations.

Get started

There are many different types of micro-organisms that can be investigated in a laboratory. Some of them are useful but some of them are very dangerous.

Throughout history we have developed ways to help our bodies fight diseases more effectively. This is a result of gaining an understanding of how diseases are spread and also how the human body naturally defends itself.

Practice

1 What is a micro-organism?

2 Explain the main difference between the way bacteria and viruses reproduce.

3 What do we call something that causes disease?

4 How are diseases transmitted by vectors?

Challenge

5 When surgeons carry out operations they have to make sure that their instruments are sterile.

   a What is meant by *sterile* in this context?

   b What type of radiation do hospitals use to sterilise surgical instruments?

   c How can you sterilise instruments in a school science lab?

   d Why do you need to sterilise the apparatus before you carry out an experiment using micro-organisms?

   e Why do you need to sterilise the apparatus after the experiment?

6 a Why did we discover bacteria much earlier than we discovered viruses?

   b Explain why you wouldn't be able to grow a virus colony on agar jelly.

   c What are the main constituents of a virus?

7 Putting food in the fridge makes it last longer before it starts to go off. Why?

8 The human body has several ways to prevent micro-organisms entering it.

a What is the most obvious barrier to micro-organisms?

b Explain the function of lysozyme in tears and sweat.

c Where are the most vulnerable places to infection in the human body?

d How does mucus help in preventing infections?

e Explain the purpose of the ciliated epithelial cells lining the air passages to the lungs.

f How do platelets in the blood help prevent infections?

9 This diagram shows discs covered in different antibiotics on a plate of agar jelly.

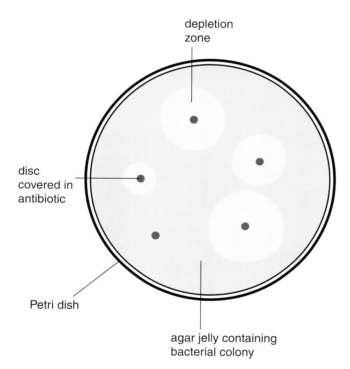

depletion zone

disc covered in antibiotic

Petri dish

agar jelly containing bacterial colony

a Relate how Fleming discovered penicillin using similar apparatus.

b How does the diagram show that some antibiotics kill bacteria?

c Which antibiotic is the most effective in this case?

d Why couldn't this antibiotic be used for all types of bacterial infection?

e Explain why it is important to finish a course of antibiotics even if you are feeling better.

Teacher's tips

It is well worth getting clear in your mind the difference between an **antiseptic** and a **disinfectant**. An antiseptic is a chemical that kills pathogens and is non toxic to the body. A disinfectant is a chemical that kills pathogens and is toxic to the body. It should not be used for external or internal body use.

18: Investigating habitats

You will revise:
- methods for obtaining organisms from a habitat
- using transects to study a habitat
- sampling techniques to estimate population size
- analysing populations.

Get started

Ecologists have developed several techniques to help study habitats. These include methods of obtaining organisms to study and ways to estimate the population sizes.

Practice

1. What is sampling? Why do you need it to estimate a population size?

2. How do you make a transect? What is it used for?

3. What is a pyramid of numbers?

Challenge

4. This diagram shows two methods for collecting small animals.

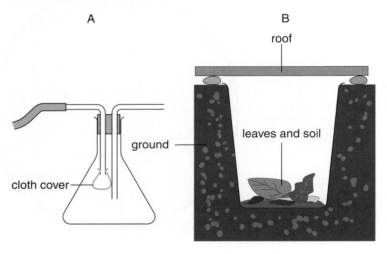

a. What is the name of each piece of apparatus?

b. Explain why apparatus B might be better at ensuring the sample is completely random.

c. State two advantages of using apparatus A rather than B.

5. a. What is the difference between population size and population density?

b. Random sampling of a habitat finds three snails for every 100 square metres. What is the population density of the snails?

c. Why are animals likely to be found in clusters rather than evenly spread throughout the habitat?

6 This sketch shows a square metre of habitat using a quadrat.

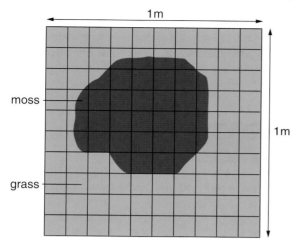

a What sort of animals can be sampled using quadrats?

b Estimate the percentage of grass in this square metre.

c Estimate the percentage of moss.

d Why would it be very difficult to count the number of organisms?

e What would you have to do in order to get a good estimate of the cover of grass and moss in the whole habitat?

7 This graph shows how the populations of foxes and rabbits change with time in a particular habitat.

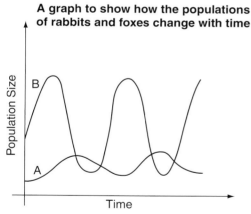

a Which graph represents the fox population? Explain your answer.

b Explain the shape of the graph. Start by assuming the population of the rabbits starts to increase.

Teacher's tips

Examination questions often ask why it is important to carry our **random sampling**. This is because it removes **bias**. Your answer must include the word bias to score well. Random sampling removes bias.

19: Atoms and elements

You will revise:
- what is meant by an element
- the symbols and properties of some common elements
- the periodic table.

Get started

All material is made out of particles called atoms. Chemicals made from only one type of atom are called elements. There are about one hundred of them. Elements with similar properties can be grouped together in the periodic table.

Practice

1 Can one element be changed into another element using chemical reactions?

2 If there are only about a hundred elements, why are there so many different types of material?

3 State one difference between a metal and a non-metal.

4 Bromine is a liquid at room temperature; name the only other element that is also in this state.

Challenge

5 Elements are identified by their name (in any particular language) and their symbol.

  a Why is it useful to have a symbol for a particular element?

  b Explain why some symbols have two letters and other symbols have one. Give an example of two elements where this occurs.

  c Why do some elements have a symbol that is not the first one or two letters of their name?

  d Identify these elements from their symbols.

    i H   ii Li   iii Ar   iv Na

    v K   vi Au   vii Hg   viii Sb

  e Write down the symbols for these elements.

    i Helium   ii Calcium   iii Magnesium

    iv Chlorine   v Lead   vi Tin

  f Which of the elements in part **e** are metals and which are non-metals?

6 Three elements are magnetic. Which are they?

7 Here is the first main row of the periodic table.

Li	Be	B	C	N	O	F	Ne

a Which of these elements are solid and which are gases at room temperature?

b Identify the two metals and five non-metals.

c Which element is neither a metal nor a non-metal? What do we call this class of element?

d Which two of these elements can be found in large quantities in the air?

e Which element is the main building block for organisms?

f Why is it rare to find the element fluorine by itself in nature?

8 Here is the first group of the periodic table and some of the characteristics of the elements.

Element	pH of oxide	Behaviour in water	Type of element	Melting point (°C)
Li	alkaline	Bubbles	Reactive metal	181
Na	alkaline	Bubbles vigorously	Reactive metal	98
K	alkaline	Bubbles and catches fire	Reactive metal	63
Rb	alkaline	Vigorously catches fire	Reactive metal	39
Cs	alkaline	Explodes (even reacts with very cold ice)	Reactive metal	28

a What information suggests that these elements are similar?

b Explain what happens to the reactivity of the elements as you go down the group.

c Which elements could possibly be in liquid form if kept outside in very hot weather?

d This group is called the alkali metals. What are the names of groups II, VII and 0?

How did I do?

I can explain what is meant by an element. ☐

I can identify where metals and non-metals lie in the periodic table. ☐

I can recognise the symbols of the common elements. ☐

I can state the physical properties of the common elements. ☐

Teacher's tips

You will not have to remember the periodic table but it is useful to familiarise yourself with its layout so that you can get most benefit from it when answering examination questions. The **horizontal rows** are called **periods** and the elements show a gradual change across each period. The **vertical columns** are called **groups** and contain elements with similar properties.

20: Molecules and compounds

You will revise:

- the difference between elements and compounds
- how elements in a compound are always in a fixed proportion
- chemical reactions involving the formation of compounds from elements.
- how symbols and numbers can be used to describe a compound
- the meaning of symbol equations
- balancing symbol equations.

Get started

When atoms bond together you get a molecule. Chemicals made from different types of atoms bonded together are called compounds. You can make compounds from elements using chemical reactions.

Elements and compounds can be represented by chemical formulae. These consist of the symbols of the elements involved. There are also numbers indicating the number of each atom in a molecule or the proportion of the elements in a compound.

Practice

1   What is the difference between elements and compounds?

2   Explain how many elements are in a molecule of water.

3   State the formulae for sulfur dioxide and hydrochloric acid.

4   The formula for ammonium sulfate is $(NH_4)_2SO_4$. Assuming you have the minimum possible number of atoms, how many atoms of each element are present?

Challenge

5   a   Explain the safety precautions you need to take when you burn magnesium in pure oxygen.

   b   What compound is being formed?

   c   Write down the word equation for this reaction.

6   Here is some apparatus for collecting chlorine from sea water.

   a   The gas from one of the electrodes is chlorine. Where does the chlorine originally come from?

   b   The gas from the other electrode gave a squeaky pop when a lighted splint was applied. What type of gas is this?

   c   Where did the gas discussed in part b originally come from?

   d   A solution of sodium hydroxide remains in the water. Write a word equation for the whole reaction.

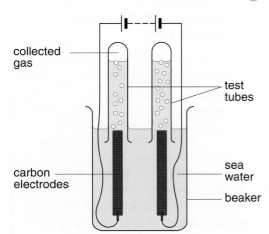

collected gas

test tubes

carbon electrodes

sea water

beaker

7 The symbol for silicon dioxide is SiO_2. It does not form molecules but the atoms are joined together in a giant structure. What does the '2' mean in this context?

8 **a** Here is a diagram of a molecule of propane. Write down the chemical formula for this compound.

Key: H = Hydrogen atom

C = Carbon atom

b Pentane has five carbon atoms in a chain (with the corresponding hydrogen atoms added as in part **a**). What would the chemical formula be for pentane?

9 When you write symbol equations to represent chemical reactions, you have to be sure that the reactions are balanced by writing numbers in front of the terms. This means that the same number of atoms has to be represented on both sides of the equation.

Here is an example: $2Mg + O_2 \rightarrow 2MgO$

Balance these equations.

a $CO_2 + C \rightarrow CO$

b $TiCl_4 + Na \rightarrow Ti + NaCl$

c $Ca(OH)_2 + HCl \rightarrow CaCl_2 + H_2O$

d $H_2 + O_2 \rightarrow H_2O$

e $Fe_2O_3 + Al \rightarrow Fe + Al_2O_3$

f $ZnS + O_2 \rightarrow ZnO + SO_2$

g $Fe_2O_3 + CO \rightarrow Fe + CO_2$

How did I do?

	✔
I can explain the difference between a compound and a mixture.	☐
I understand that some compounds consist of a giant structure rather than individual molecules.	☐
I can do calculations based on the fixed proportions of compounds.	☐
I can describe the structure of a molecule from its chemical formula.	☐
I can write down the chemical formula of a molecule based on its description.	☐
I can balance simple symbol equations.	☐

Teacher's tips

Chemical equations must be balanced. There must be the same number of atoms either side of the arrow.

When checking that an equation is balanced it is a good idea to write the number of each type of atom underneath the equation and check both side are the same.

$C_6 H_{12} O_6 + 6O_2 \rightarrow 6CO_2 + 6H_2O$

$C = 6\ H = 12\ O = 18 \rightarrow C = 6\ H = 12\ O = 18$

21: Mixtures

You will revise:

- the difference between a compound and a mixture
- how to separate mixtures by fractional distillation
- how mixtures affect cooling curves.

Get started

Mixtures of elements and compounds are not chemically combined and can be separated by physical means. Compounds and mixtures also behave differently when they are changing state.

Practice

1 Is a solution a compound or a mixture?

2 Explain why the elements in a compound are always in fixed proportions but the proportions in a mixture can vary.

3 What is meant by the decomposition of a compound? Write the word equation for the decomposition of silver chloride when light shines on it.

Challenge

4 Is air a compound or a mixture?

5 Obtaining the individual gases from the air is an expensive process. Choose two of the gases present and explain why they are useful.

6 Here is a graph showing the cooling curve for a mixture of tin and lead.

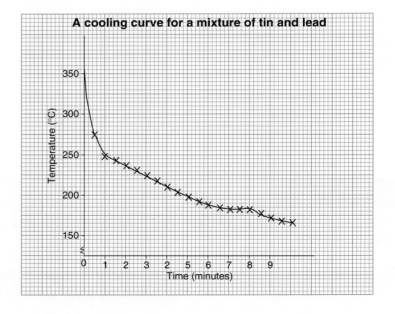

A cooling curve for a mixture of tin and lead

a Why couldn't you carry out this experiment in a school laboratory?

b The lead starts to freeze before the tin. At what temperature does this happen?

c What happens to the concentration of the tin in the liquid mixture after the lead begins to freeze?

d At what temperature does the whole mixture completely freeze?

e The melting point of lead is 327 °C and the melting point of tin is 232 °C. What do you notice about your answer to part d?

f A tin/lead mix has been used by plumbers for soldering pipes together. Explain why a wide-ranging melting point is useful in this instance.

7 Amalgams, alloys, gels and aerosols are all different types of mixtures. Find out what particular mixtures these terms refer to.

8 In terms of the particles involved, suggest why a mixture of tin and lead freezes at a lower temperature than the freezing temperature of either of the two substances.

How did I do?

I can explain why it is easier to separate mixtures than compounds. ✔ ☐

I can write about the gases found in air and how they are separated. ☐

I can discuss the main features of the cooling curve for a tin/lead mix. ☐

I can state other examples of mixtures such as aerosols and gels. ☐

Teacher's tips

Because mixtures are made of substances that are present together but are not combined the constituent parts can be separated. There are several separation techniques and it is worth learning the main stages involved in each one – they are: **filtration**, **evaporation**, **chromatography**, **distillation** and **fractional distillation**.

22: Weathering of rocks

You will revise:
- the relationship between rocks and minerals
- an experiment to calculate the porosity of rocks
- different types of physical, chemical and biological weathering.

Get started

Over time rocks are gradually broken into smaller pieces by the effect of weathering. This process is an important part of the rock cycle. It also means that minerals end up in the soil.

Practice

1 Explain the difference between rocks and minerals.

2 State which of these materials are made from rock: fossils, grains of sand, clay, peat and diamond.

3 What is the difference between weathering and erosion?

4 Explain what is meant by physical and chemical weathering.

Challenge

5 a Unusually, what happens to the volume of water when it freezes?

b Explain how this can lead to weathering of porous rocks.

c What climate causes this type of weathering to happen the quickest?

6 A pupil did an experiment to find the porosity of some chalk. He placed a piece of chalk into 60 cm^3 of water in a measuring cylinder. The volume of the water rose to 85 cm^3. After 3 days the water level had decreased to 82 cm^3.

a What is the volume of the chalk?

b How much water did the chalk absorb? What have you assumed?

c The porosity is calculated by dividing the volume of water absorbed by the volume of the rock and then multiplying by 100. Calculate the porosity of the chalk.

The pupil repeated the experiment with a sample of granite. He found the porosity to be 1%.

d Which sample, the chalk or the granite, will weather the quickest if the weathering is due to the expansion of water?

e Explain how the different structures of chalk and granite lead to such different porosities.

f Which of these rocks would be more useful at the bed of a reservoir?

7   **a**   In the desert, there is a large difference in temperature between the day and the night. Explain how this might lead to the weathering of desert rocks.

   b   Why might a stone building in the middle of a forest need restoration earlier than a similar building that isn't in a forest? What is this type of weathering called?

8   This question is about the chemical weathering of rocks.

   a   What natural phenomenon leads to water dissolving carbon dioxide?

   b   The acid formed from water and carbon dioxide is called carbonic acid (H_2CO_3). Write a symbol equation for this reaction.

Carbonic acid reacts with limestone to form calcium hydrogen carbonate. Here is the reaction:

$$H_2CO_3 + CaCO_3 \rightarrow Ca(HCO_3)_2$$

   c   Write the name of the compound that limestone is made from.

   d   Calcium hydrogen carbonate is soluble in water. Explain how this leads to the erosion of limestone.

   e   Pollution from burning fossil fuels can increase levels of sulfur dioxide in the atmosphere. Explain how this can accelerate the rate of weathering.

9   The chemical reaction between carbonic acid and limestone in question **8** is reversible. Explain how this reaction can first lead to cave formations and then to stalactites and stalagmites.

10   By referring to the method of weathering in question **9**, explain why rocks get weaker and weaker with every cycle of freezing and thawing. What happens to the size of the cracks and the number of cracks? Why doesn't the rock break apart immediately?

11   Explain why rocks that have recently emerged from the Earth's crust already have cracks in them, even when no weathering has taken place.

How did I do?

	✔
I can explain the difference between rocks and minerals.	☐
I can explain measure the porosity of rocks.	☐
I can explain how the expansion of water can weather rocks.	☐
I can summarise the physical, chemical and biological processes of weathering.	☐

Teacher's tips

The weathering of rocks brings together many topics you have already covered and it is worth taking a moment to reflect on these and see how they relate to each other.

- **physical weathering** occurs as a result of rocks heating up by day and cooling at night
- **chemical weathering** is the result of acid rain
- **biological weathering** involves animal and plant activity which weaken the rocks.

23: The rock cycle

You will revise:
- extrusive and intrusive igneous rocks
- the role of temperature in the formation of igneous rocks
- the movement of material around the rock cycle.

Get started

Over millions of years, the materials that make up the rocks go round in a big cycle. Imagine what sort of journey a calcium atom might have made before it ends up in your bones.

Practice

1 How do the materials in igneous rocks end up in sedimentary rocks?

2 What do we call underground molten rock?

3 State two conditions that are needed to change metamorphic rocks into igneous rocks.

4 Why don't rocks have fixed melting points?

Challenge

5 **a** Use the particle model of matter to explain why crystals form when magma cools.

b What type of rock is produced in this process?

c Explain why the sizes of the crystals indicate the conditions under which the rock was made.

d Manufacturers want to grow very large silicon crystals which they can then cut up to make silicon chips for computers. Suggest how they might grow these crystals.

6 Here is a diagram of a volcano.

a Why are there layers of igneous rock?

b Where would you find metamorphic rock in this diagram?

7 **a** Explain why extrusive igneous rocks are likely to have much smaller crystals than intrusive rocks.

b Why can pumice float on water?

c Suggest one piece of evidence that pumice is an extrusive igneous rock.

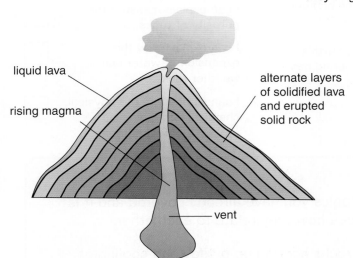

liquid lava

rising magma

alternate layers of solidified lava and erupted solid rock

vent

8 Here is a table showing some data about different igneous rocks.

Type of rock	Intrusive or extrusive	Density (g/cm³)
Granite	Intrusive	2.7
Gabbro	Intrusive	3.0
Rhyolite	Extrusive	2.7
Basalt	Extrusive	3.0

a State which rock has the same chemical composition as gabbro.

b Identify two of these rocks that are relatively silica rich and two that are relatively iron rich.

c Suggest which type of rock is found in continental crust and which is found in oceanic crust (which lies lower down in the mantle).

9 Copy and complete this schematic diagram of the rock cycle.

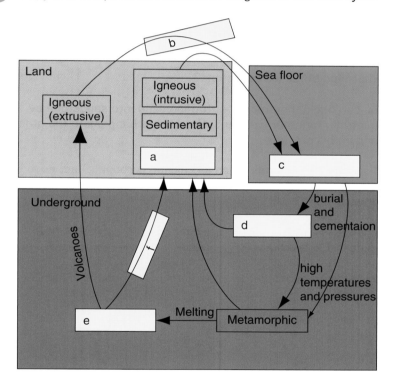

Teacher's tips

The rock cycle relates to the changes that take place over millions of years as one form changes into another. You will see many different versions of a rock cycle drawing in textbooks. Draw one for yourself and learn it. The rock cycle is a popular examination question.

24: Types of rock

You will revise:
- the three main types of rock
- how each type is formed
- the main differences between them.

Get started

There are three main types of rock: igneous, sedimentary and metamorphic. They are all formed in different ways.

Practice

1. Which types of rock contain fossils?

2. Metamorphic rocks can be formed from which types of rock?

3. Under what conditions are metamorphic rocks produced?

4. Why are metamorphic rocks generally much harder than sedimentary rocks?

Challenge

5. a What type of rock is sandstone?

   b You can begin the process of turning sand into sandstone by squeezing together wet sand. State what happens to the grains of sand in this process.

   c In sandstone, minerals (such as calcium carbonate) act as a matrix holding the sand particles together. Describe how this matrix is formed.

   d A geode is a hollow rock containing large crystals that have grown inside it. Explain how these crystals have been produced.

6. Here is a diagram of layers of sedimentary rock found in a valley in Namibia.

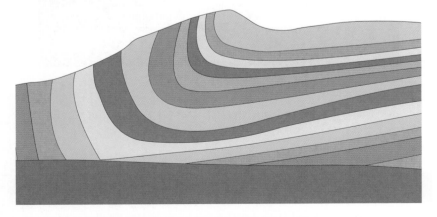

   a Suggest what might have happened to produce this formation.

b Why is it likely that you will find some metamorphic rocks in this area?

c Explain why the same sedimentary rock turns into different types of metamorphic rock at different temperatures and pressures.

7 **a** In terms of their chemical composition, state one feature that all types of limestone have in common.

b In what way are different types of limestone different?

8 **a** Which type of metamorphic rock does limestone turn into?

Shale turns into slate at high temperatures and pressures.

b State two properties of slate that makes it useful for building roofs.

c State two features about the grains in shale that change when slate is formed.

d Why are the fossils found in slate often distorted?

e At higher temperatures and pressures, slate changes into phyllite, schist and finally gneiss. These rocks contain different minerals to the ones originally in the slate. Explain how these different minerals were formed.

9 **a** How is igneous rock formed?

b What is meant by intrusive and extrusive igneous rock?

10 For each rock listed, state whether it is sedimentary, metamorphic or igneous.

a Basalt	**b** Marble	**c** Granite
d Limestone	**e** Shale	**f** Slate
g Pumice	**h** Schist	**i** Gabbro

11 A very rare type of rock found on Earth's surface hasn't been formed by any of the processes you have investigated. What type of rock is this?

12 Why do over 90% of rocks contain silicates?

13 Explain why in some places metamorphic rocks only occur in small areas but in other places you get vast regions of metamorphic rocks.

How did I do?

I can write down the three main types of rock and how they were formed. ✔ ☐

I can explain why metamorphic rock is much denser than sedimentary rock. ☐

I can suggest likely places to find igneous and metamorphic rocks. ☐

Teacher's tips

It is vital that you know the names of the three main types of rock you need to be familiar with (igneous, sedimentary and metamorphic). You need to know the **characteristics** and a **named example** of each type. The only way to achieve this is to sit and learn them.

25: Heat and temperature

You will revise:
- the need for a temperature scale
- how differences in temperature govern the transfer of heat energy
- the roles of temperature and heat energy when objects change state.
- the three main methods of heat transfer
- how to explain conduction and convection in terms of particles
- how we can reduce heat transfer using insulating materials.

Get started

Although we can describe things we feel as hot or cold, we need to use a temperature scale to make proper scientific measurements. Transferring heat energy can make objects hotter or colder and it can also make them change their state.

Heat is transferred from hotter objects to colder objects. The rate at which the heat is transferred depends on the temperature difference and on the 'ease' with which the transfer takes place. There are three main methods of heat transfer: conduction, convection and radiation.

Practice

1 Describe an experiment where your left hand feels a bowl of water as hot, while your right hand feels the same water as cold.

2 What is the unit by which we measure heat?

3 Explain what is meant by insulation.

4 A string vest contains lots of holes. How do the holes keep the wearer warm?

5 Explain how a vacuum flask can keep hot things hot and cold things cold.

6 Why can you only get convection in liquids and gases?

Challenge

7 You have a bowl of crushed ice in water.

   a What temperature would this bowl be (at normal atmospheric pressure)?

   b At first, what would happen to the crushed ice and water if you transferred heat energy away from the bowl (by placing it in a freezer)?

   c How could you tell if the temperature falls below the value you stated in part a simply by looking at the bowl?

   d If, instead, you were transferring heat energy to the bowl, how could you tell when the temperature goes above this value?

   e What similar situation occurs at 100 °C?

   f Describe how you could add a scale to an alcohol thermometer to measure the temperature in centigrade.

8 When liquids freeze to become solids, they give heat energy out without reducing their temperature. Where does this heat energy come from?

9 If you plot the temperature of a hot mug of coffee against time, you get a cooling curve. Why does the graph curve?

10 You have a steel rod. One end of the rod is hot and the other end is cold.

    a What form of energy is affected by how fast objects are moving?

    b Describe how this type of energy varies along the rod.

    c After a while, heat has conducted along the rod so that the rod is all at the same temperature. Rewrite your answer to part **b** for this new situation.

    d Explain how the heat energy has been transferred along the rod.

11 Here is a diagram of some water and ice being heated in a test tube.

    a Explain the purpose of the gauze.

    b The top of the water is boiling, while the bottom of the tube is still cold. What does this tell you about the water?

    c Why wouldn't this experiment work in a copper container?

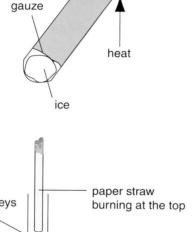

12 This diagram shows some smoke being drawn through a glass chimney.

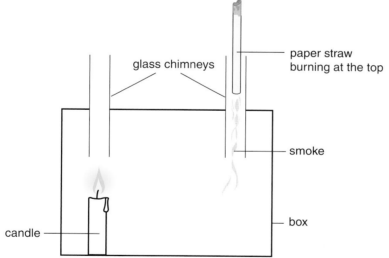

    a Explain why the smoke moves down through the chimney.

    b If the straw was placed above the other chimney, what would happen?

    c What do we call this method of heat transfer?

13 An essential source of energy on the Earth is heat energy from the Sun. Explain why there must be another method of heat transfer other than conduction and convection.

14 Why are metals such good conductors of heat?

15 How do most methods of house insulation work?

Teacher's tips

Once you understand the main principles of conduction, convection and radiation you can start applying them to everyday situations.

A popular **examination question** relates to the **heat losses** that occur from a **house** and ways to **prevent** such losses. For example, placing a draught excluder around the main door into a house, and the windows, reduces the heat losses due to convection. Find out other ways heat is lost, and how to minimize them, so that you are fully prepared to answer the application-type questions you will encounter.

26: Magnetism

You will revise:
- magnets and magnetic materials
- the domain theory of magnetism
- magnetic fields produced by current-carrying wires and solenoids.

Get started

Magnets, magnetic materials and wires carrying electric currents feel forces acting on them when they are inside a magnetic field. The nature of this force can be explored by using ideas about magnetic poles, field lines and domains.

Practice

1 Which of these materials are magnetic and which are non-magnetic: tin, cobalt, mercury, nickel, iron oxide, iron sulfide?

2 Write down the combinations of poles that attract and the combinations of poles that repel.

3 Why is one end of a bar magnet called a N pole?

4 What is the difference between a magnet and a magnetic material?

Challenge

5 A pupil investigated some metal bars (A to F) that looked exactly the same. Her teacher asked her to identify whether the bars were magnetic, made out of magnetic material (but not magnetised) or not made of a magnetic material at all. From her results below, identify the category of each bar.

Bar A attracted some iron filings (the filings weren't magnetised).

Bar A attracted bar B.

Bar A repelled bar C.

Bar D turned and pointed due north when it was suspended in the air.

Bar B didn't pick up any iron filings.

Bar E didn't point due north when suspended in the air but a small compass did point towards it.

Bar F wasn't attracted by bar D and it didn't pick up any iron filings.

Teacher's tips

Make sure you can name the three metallic elements that have magnetic properties:

- **nickel (Ni)**
- **iron (Fe)**
- **cobalt (Co)**

6 One model of magnetic materials describes them as having lots of tiny magnets (called domains) inside. Each tiny magnet can be represented by an arrow, with the arrow head representing the N pole.

    a Here are some diagrams representing three magnetic materials. Which one is unmagnetised, which is slightly magnetised and which is completely magnetised?

A
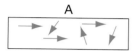

B
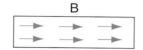

C

    b Why is there a limit to how strongly you can magnetise some iron?

    c Why does heating a magnet make it lose its magnetism?

7   **a** What is a magnetic field?

    b Which direction do field lines point: towards the N pole of the magnet or towards the S pole?

    c How can you tell, by looking at the field lines, where the magnetic field is the strongest?

    d How does the strength of a magnetic field change as the distance increases?

    e If Earth's magnetic field was produced by a bar magnet, which pole of the magnet would be pointing due north?

    f Sketch the shape of the magnetic field produced by the Earth.

8 Here are two magnetic fields produced by current-carrying wires. What is the arrangement of the wires that have produced them?

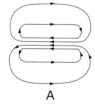

A

B

9 One way of magnetising a magnetic material is to point the material due north and hammer it very gently. How does this work?

10 A current-carrying solenoid produces a weak magnetic field. Why does placing an iron nail inside the solenoid make the magnetic field much stronger?

27: Using magnetism

You will revise:
- electromagnets
- buzzers and bells
- relays and circuit breakers.

Get started

An electromagnet enables you to turn magnetic forces on and off at the flick of a switch. This has resulted in many useful devices.

Practice

1. What are the basic components of an electromagnet?

2. State two things you can do to make an electromagnet stronger.

3. How could you change the S pole of an electromagnet into a N pole without moving it?

4. What happens to the electromagnet when you turn the current off?

Challenge

5. a What is the difference between an a.c. and a d.c. current?

   b What is happening to an a.c. current for the split second that it is at 0 A?

   c Describe how you can use this effect to make a buzzer using an electromagnet and a springy steel blade.

   d Explain why an electromagnet connected to an a.c. supply can still pick up a steel paper clip.

6. a What is a relay? What is it used for?

   b The diagram shows part of a relay. Explain how it works.

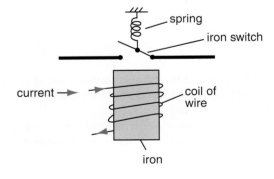

7 A pupil adapts the relay shown in question **6** to make a model of a circuit breaker. He turns the switch upside down and places the spring above the switch. This means that the spring keeps the switch closed when the electromagnet is off but when the current is supplied to the electromagnet, it tries to pull the switch open against the pull of the spring.

    a Circuit breakers are safety devices that break the circuit if the current gets too large. Explain how this one might work.

    b What would happen if the current supplied to the electromagnet did stop flowing? Why would this be a potential problem for this design of circuit breaker?

8 Here is a diagram of an electric bell.

    a When the switch is closed, what happens to the electromagnet?

    b How does this result in the hammer striking the gong?

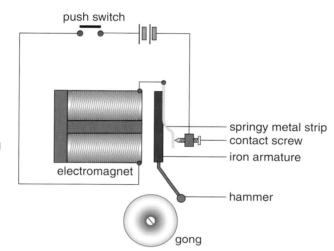

    c Why does the electromagnet switch off at this stage?

    d What happens to the hammer once the electromagnet has switched off?

    e Why does the electromagnet switch back on again?

    f Explain how the hammer continues to repetitively strike the gong.

9 What is the difference between a soft and a hard magnetic material? So why is iron used in electromagnets rather than steel?

10 Why does the melting temperature of copper wire limit the strength of electromagnets? How can superconductors solve this problem?

11 By mistake a pupil winding the wire round an iron nail starts winding in the opposite direction halfway along the nail. In terms of the domains in the iron explain why the electromagnet won't work.

How did I do?

I can suggest and explain two things you can do to make an electromagnet stronger. ✔ ☐

Given a diagram of an electric bell, I can explain how it works. ☐

I can describe how a relay and a circuit breaker work. ☐

Teacher's tips

Examination questions frequently ask students to give an example of a **use** of an **electromagnet** – so learn this one!

The bodies of many cars contain steel. Steel is a metal alloy which can show magnetic properties. A large electromagnet is used in a scrap yard to move the steel bodies of cars from place to place.

28: Light and reflection

You will revise:
- the nature of light and how it travels
- angles of incidence and reflection
- images in mirrors.

Get started

Light is a special kind of electromagnetic wave that we can detect when it enters our eyes. It moves very quickly in straight lines and it interacts with different materials in different ways.

Practice

1 What is the special name that we give to the speed that light travels in a vacuum?

2 Explain the difference between a transparent and a translucent material.

3 What type of materials form shadows?

4 Where do we see the image in a mirror: in front of it, on its surface, or behind it?

Challenge

5 A teacher sets up a demonstration of a laser beam.

   a What safety precautions should you take when using a laser?

   b Explain why pupils could only see the patch of light where the laser beam hit the wall rather than the beam itself.

   c The teacher then sprayed some deodorant into the room. Explain why pupils could now observe the beam.

   d What shape of path did the beam follow?

6 Light can be both transmitted and reflected at the surface of a piece of glass such as a shop window.

   a If both transmission and reflection take place, what do you see when you look through the window into the shop?

   b Why does the inside of the shop look a lot clearer when you are looking through the window at night time (assuming the shop lights are on)?

   c The shopkeeper fitted windows that didn't absorb as much light. How did the view looking into the shop change?

7 This diagram shows how a ray of light from a raybox is reflected by a mirror.

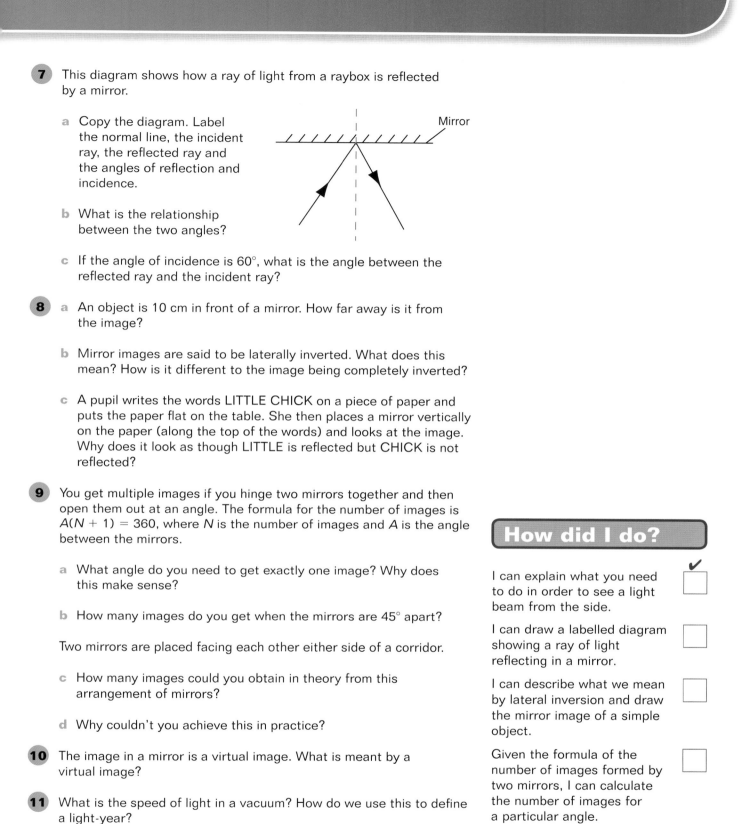

a Copy the diagram. Label the normal line, the incident ray, the reflected ray and the angles of reflection and incidence.

b What is the relationship between the two angles?

c If the angle of incidence is 60°, what is the angle between the reflected ray and the incident ray?

8 a An object is 10 cm in front of a mirror. How far away is it from the image?

b Mirror images are said to be laterally inverted. What does this mean? How is it different to the image being completely inverted?

c A pupil writes the words LITTLE CHICK on a piece of paper and puts the paper flat on the table. She then places a mirror vertically on the paper (along the top of the words) and looks at the image. Why does it look as though LITTLE is reflected but CHICK is not reflected?

9 You get multiple images if you hinge two mirrors together and then open them out at an angle. The formula for the number of images is $A(N + 1) = 360$, where N is the number of images and A is the angle between the mirrors.

a What angle do you need to get exactly one image? Why does this make sense?

b How many images do you get when the mirrors are 45° apart?

Two mirrors are placed facing each other either side of a corridor.

c How many images could you obtain in theory from this arrangement of mirrors?

d Why couldn't you achieve this in practice?

10 The image in a mirror is a virtual image. What is meant by a virtual image?

11 What is the speed of light in a vacuum? How do we use this to define a light-year?

How did I do?

I can explain what you need to do in order to see a light beam from the side. ✔ ☐

I can draw a labelled diagram showing a ray of light reflecting in a mirror. ☐

I can describe what we mean by lateral inversion and draw the mirror image of a simple object. ☐

Given the formula of the number of images formed by two mirrors, I can calculate the number of images for a particular angle. ☐

Teacher's tips

You must make sure that when you draw your own ray diagrams you use a **pencil**, **ruler** and **protractor**. Construct your diagram as accurately as possible. You must measure the angles carefully and know the terms **incident ray** and **reflected ray**.

29: Refraction and colour

You will revise:
- refraction
- separating white light into the visible spectrum
- colour mixing.

Get started

Light rays can change speed when they pass from one medium to another. This makes them change direction if they pass through the interface at an angle. Different colours of light bend by different amounts, which means that white light splits into the visible spectrum when it passes through a triangular prism.

Practice

1 What is meant by refraction?

2 State the name given to the phenomenon of splitting light up into its constituent colours.

3 Explain the difference between primary and secondary colours.

4 When you shine white light onto a pair of blue jeans, why do they look blue?

Challenge

5 The diagram below shows a ray of light entering a glass block.

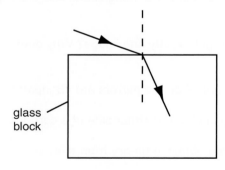

glass block

a Copy the diagram and label the incident ray, the refracted ray, the normal line and the angles of refraction and incidence.

b What also happens to the light ray at the interface?

c Why does the light ray change direction?

d In general, what is different about the angle of refraction and the angle of incidence for rays entering a glass block?

e What is the special case where the angle of incidence equals the angle of refraction?

6 Explain why a swimming pool looks shallower than it actually is.

7 **a** Why does white light split into several colours when it passes through a triangular prism.

b What is the name given to the band of colours produced from this effect?

c How did Newton use a second prism to show that the green light from the visible spectrum was a pure colour?

8 A teacher shone overlapping circles of red, green and blue light onto a screen. The diagram shows what the screen looked like.

Copy the diagram and fill in the missing colours.

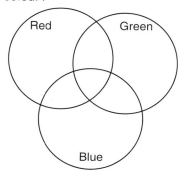

9 Explain why a magenta pair of trousers looks blue when they are in cyan-coloured light.

10 Copy and complete this table about the appearance of different coloured clothes in different coloured lights.

Colour of clothing (in white light)	Colour in red light	Colour in blue light	Colour in green light	Colour in yellow light	Colour in cyan light	Colour in magenta light
Red	Red	Black		Red	Black	
Blue						
Green						
Yellow						
Cyan						

11 What is the difference between compound yellow and pure yellow light?

12 What colour would a red shirt appear in pure yellow light?

13 Why do our eyes perceive pure yellow and compound yellow as the same colour?

Teacher's tips

Do not mix up the terms **reflection** and **refraction**. Reflection is what happens when light bounces off a surface and refraction is the bending of light as it passes from air into glass or water.

30: Sound waves

You will revise:
- ▶ how sound is produced and how sound waves travel
- ▶ using an oscilloscope to represent a sound wave
- ▶ the effect of altering pitch and volume on the shape of a sound wave.

Get started

Vibrations can travel through the air or another medium as sound.
The nature of these vibrations determines what sort of sound we hear.

Practice

1 Why can't sound waves pass through a vacuum?

2 How does the speed of sound vary in solids, liquids and gases?

3 What is the frequency of a sound wave? What unit is it measured in?

4 How does the amplitude of a wave vary if it is carrying more energy?

Challenge

5 a What do the strings of a guitar have to do in order to produce sound?

b State two things you can do to make a guitar string produce a higher pitched note.

c How else do the different guitar strings produce the different pitches?

6 This diagram shows traces of sound waves on an oscilloscope screen.

A ⟿⟿⟿   B ⁓⁓⁓   C ∿∿∿∿   D ∿

a Which trace has the highest frequency?

b Which traces are from sounds at the same pitch?

c Describe the sound that is producing trace D.

d Which traces have the same amplitude?

e How do the sounds producing traces B and C differ?

f If the microphone connected to trace A is moved further away from the sound source, how would the trace change? Without altering the sound, how could you make the trace look the same again?

7 A sitar and a harp produce two notes at the same pitch and volume yet they sound very different.

    a State two similarities between the two sound waves they produce.

    b How would the oscilloscope traces differ?

8 A hydrophone is a device that can pick up sounds under water. Here is a diagram of a simple one that you can make.

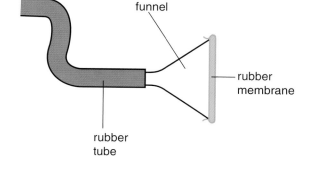

funnel

rubber membrane

rubber tube

    a Describe, in terms of the particles involved, how the sound from the water is carried through the hydrophone.

    b How does the funnel help to amplify the sound?

    c In which direction do the air particles vibrate in the rubber tube?

    d Explain why you can't hear an underwater animal when your ear is above the surface of the water but you can hear it quite clearly when your ear is under the water.

9 **a** Explain why the speed of sound in solids is faster than it is in liquids.

    b Why can you hear that a train is coming for a long time before it actually appears?

    c Why can whale song be heard over a much greater distance in water than in air?

    d Why does the sound produced by an earthquake arrive at exactly the same time as the actual earthquake?

10 When you cup your hands over your mouth, the person directly in front of you can hear you more clearly. Explain how this works.

11 Explain why a pitch at 3000 Hzs sounds louder than a pitch at 100 Hz even though the amplitude is the same. Why do babies cry at a pitch of 3000 Hz?

How did I do?

I can explain why sound travels differently in gases, liquids and solids.	✔ ☐
I can state three ways in which you can change the pitch of the sound produced by a vibrating string.	☐
I can relate pitch and volume to frequency and amplitude of a sound wave.	☐

Teacher's tips

Make sure you can draw a sound wave and label and define the key terms associated with it.

- **Amplitude** – the loudness of a sound
- **Pitch** – how high or low sound is
- **Frequency** – the number of full waves that pass a set point per second
- **Wavelength** – the distance between two identical places on an oscilloscope trace of a sound wave

31: Hearing sound

You will revise:

- the structure of the human ear and how sound energy travels through it
- problems that people can have with their hearing
- artificial aids that can help with these problems.

Get started

The ear converts vibrations in the air into electrical signals that are passed to the brain. Unfortunately some people are born with hearing impairments, and hearing can be damaged by excessive noise and ageing. Artificial aids can sometimes help.

Practice

1. What is the normal frequency range of human hearing?

2. How does this range change as you get older?

3. What scale do we use to describe the loudness of noise?

Challenge

4. Here is a diagram of the human ear.

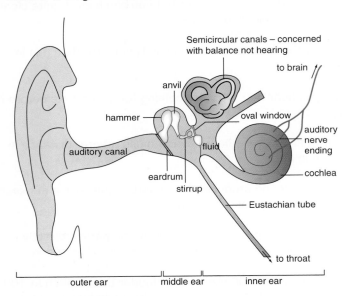

a Describe in as much detail as you can how the energy from the sound wave entering the ear ends up as an electrical signal in the auditory nerve.

b State two advantages of the outer ear being funnel shaped.

c The ossicles (hammer, anvil and stirrup) act like levers. This means that the stirrup moves much more then the hammer. Explain how this amplifies the sound.

d The ossicles also reduce the amount of reflection of the sound wave when it passes into the inner ear. Why would a lot of reflection be a problem?

e Explain the advantage of having fluid inside the ear.

f Suggest why the cochlea is spiral shaped.

5 a Some hearing devices turn sound waves into vibrations in the skull. Explain how this can help some people who have hearing impairments.

b There is a part of the ear that, if damaged, will result in a hearing impairment that can't be helped with today's technology. Which part is it?

c Most hearing aids amplify the sound electronically. Why is it important for an audiologist to test the patient's hearing at lots of different frequencies before they program a hearing aid?

6 The threshold of hearing is given a value of 0 on the decibel scale.

a What is meant by the threshold of hearing?

b If somebody has a threshold of 40 dB, can they hear sounds easily or is their hearing impaired? Explain your answer.

7 Here is a graph of how the threshold of hearing varies with frequency for a normal ear.

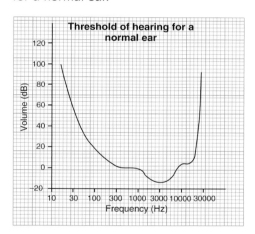

a Which frequency is the ear most sensitive to?

b Why is this important for designers of fire alarms?

c State two ways in which the graph would change for a much older person.

Teacher's tips

Learn the names of the structures that make up the outer middle and inner ear along with their functions.

- **Outer ear** – pinna and auditory canal
- **Middle ear** – ear drum, hammer, anvil and stirrup
- **Inner ear** – semi-circular canals, cochlea and auditory nerve

You will revise:

▷ inherited characteristics through sexual reproduction

▷ dominant and recessive genes

▷ what we mean by a clone and how we can produce them.

▷ environmental and genetic causes of variation

▷ natural and artificial selection

▷ the difference between a species and a breed

▷ genetic modification.

Get started

Organisms of the same species have characteristics that are different from each other. Offspring can inherit different characteristics from the same parents. Organisms that are clones of each other are genetically identical.

Variation within a species can arise from both environmental and genetic factors. Natural and artificial selection can result in some of these different characteristics passing down the generations but other characteristics can die out altogether.

Practice

1 What are gametes?

2 How are sperm and egg cells adapted for their roles in reproduction?

3 What are genes? Where would you find them in a cell?

4 Why is your genetic make-up more similar to your parents' than to your grandparents'?

5 Discuss whether the height of a tree is an inherited or an environmental characteristic.

Challenge

6 a Explain how sexual reproduction leads to offspring with characteristics from both the mother and the father.

b Why do brothers and sisters have some characteristics that are similar but other characteristics that are very different?

c Describe how fertilisation can lead to identical and non-identical twins.

d Is it possible for two sisters to have the same genetic make-up even if they are not identical twins? Explain your answer.

Teacher's tips

There are lots of **pairs** of terms in this section and it is important that you can distinguish between each pair as '**distinguish between the following two terms**' are popular examination questions.

- sexual and asexual reproduction
- dominant and recessive genes
- environmental versus genetic causes of variation
- species and breed.

7 **a** What is a clone?

b How can you clone plants?

c Explain why single-celled amoebae are clones of each other.

One way to produce a clone is to completely remove the nucleus from an egg and replace it with the nucleus from a cell of another individual. This behaves like a normal fertilised egg and, in the right conditions, will develop into a new organism.

d Is the new organism a clone of the organism that produced the egg or a clone from the organism that produced the nucleus?

e Why is it theoretically possible to produce a clone from almost any cell of your body?

f Suggest two reasons why not many mammals have been cloned so far.

8 The DNA in the nucleus of your cells is split up into pairs of chromosomes. Describe how the chromosomes determine what gender you are.

9 A farmer has a female cow that is good at producing milk, and a bull that produces a lot of meat.

a Suggest how the farmer could produce a cow that is both good at producing milk but also produces good meat over several generations.

b State one other characteristic that farmers would try to encourage by selective breeding.

10 **a** Describe how you can make clones of geraniums.

b Why would this method of producing geraniums be no good if you wanted to improve a certain characteristic (e.g. colour of flowers)?

c If you had a collection of geraniums, how might you be able to produce a new breed of geranium?

11 We have now learnt to enhance certain characteristics of crops (such as their yield or nutritional value) by genetically modifying them.

a State one similarity and one difference between genetic modification and selective breeding.

b Some people are worried about genetically modified (GM) crops. Suggest a cause for concern with using this new technology.

c State two advantages of using GM crops.

How did I do?

	✔
I can describe the difference between identical and non-identical twins in terms of their genetic make-up.	☐
I can explain how siblings can have very different characteristics even though they have the same parents.	☐
I can draw diagrams to show how we can produce a clone by replacing the nucleus of an egg.	☐
I can explain the difference between artificial and natural selection.	☐
I can suggest a breeding programme to develop a breed that has desirable characteristics.	☐
I can discuss the advantages and disadvantages of genetic modification.	☐

33: Health, diet and drugs

Get started

The body has many systems which need to work together effectively. These systems can become less effective with aging and with an unhealthy lifestyle.

Your body has to deal with any material that enters it. Most material (such as a balanced diet and prescribed drugs) does the body good. However, other material can cause harm.

Practice

1 Explain the difference between being fit and being healthy.

2 Write down the word equation and the symbol equation for respiration.

3 Briefly describe the systems of the body that deliver the reactants of respiration to the cells and then remove the products.

4 What are the similarities and differences between a stroke and a heart attack?

5 State the five principle components of a balanced diet.

6 State two factors that are leading to a more obese society. Suggest how these factors have arisen in recent years.

7 Why can drinking alcohol be far more dangerous than just a risk to long-term health?

8 What do we mean by the terms *addiction* and *tolerance* when we talk about drugs?

Challenge

9 a What organ is responsible for creating blood pressure?

b Why do people who have low blood pressure often feel faint and lack energy?

c Explain how cholesterol lining the insides of your blood vessels increases blood pressure.

d What might eventually happen to the blood vessels if you have high blood pressure?

10 This question is about the effect that smoking has on health.

    a Why do people become addicted to smoking?

    b Explain the normal function of ciliated epithelial cells that line the air passages.

    c Smoking can stop the cilia beating properly. How does this lead to a smoker's cough?

    d State two reasons why smokers can become permanently short of oxygen.

    e Some chemicals in inhaled smoke are carcinogenic. What disease could these chemicals cause?

    f Explain how a mother smoking when she is pregnant could have an adverse effect on the fetus.

11 **a** Explain how your body respires when there is not enough oxygen.

    b Why do you continue to breathe heavily for a while after you have exercised?

How did I do?

I can describe the processes of respiration and breathing and how this leads to effective cell function. ✔

I can explain the difference between muscles, tendons and ligaments and why we always need at least two muscles for a particular joint.

I can describe the biological dangers of smoking.

Teacher's tips

Examination questions often ask about the roles of the **cilia** and **mucus** in the respiratory system. It is common for students to mix up the roles of these two. Be clear that the mucus traps the dirt and germs breathed in and the cilia waft the mucus, with trapped substances, up to the back of the throat from where it can be swallowed into the stomach.

34: Photosynthesis

You will revise:
- the chemical reaction of photosynthesis
- experimental evidence for photosynthesis
- factors that affect the rate of the reaction.

Get started

Plants can convert energy from the Sun into chemical energy by photosynthesis. The plants themselves use this energy in respiration but some of the energy is passed up the food chain. As well as providing us with energy in a useful form it also produces the oxygen we breathe.

Practice

1 Photosynthesis can be split up into two words: *photo* and *synthesis*. Explain how these words describe the chemical reaction.

2 Describe the standard tests for oxygen, carbon dioxide and starch.

3 How are photosynthesis and respiration related?

4 What is meant by biomass?

Challenge

5 **a** Write down the word equation and the symbol equation for photosynthesis.

b This reaction needs energy to work. Where does this energy come from?

c In terms of the energy involved, explain the role of the chlorophyll in the leaves.

6 This question is about growing an orange tree in a tub of soil.

a Every year, the orange tree gains mass and the soil loses mass. However, the amount of mass the tree gains is thousands of times more than the mass the soil loses. Suggest where this extra mass has come from.

b Why does the mass of the soil decrease a little (assuming that the water content remains the same)?

7 **a** When you are carrying out experiments to investigate photosynthesis, why do you sometimes need to de-starch the plant?

b De-starching plants involves putting them in darkness for a few days. Explain what happens to the starch.

Once the plants have been de-starched you can carry out your investigation. One way of detecting photosynthesis is by looking for new starch that has been formed in the leaves.

c By considering the difference between plant cells and animal cells, explain why placing iodine on the leaves of a plant has no effect.

d How does boiling the leaves in water and then applying hot ethanol allow the iodine test to work? (Hint: chlorophyll is insoluble in water.)

e Describe how you can heat up ethanol safely.

8 Here is a diagram showing some pondweed photosynthesising in some water.

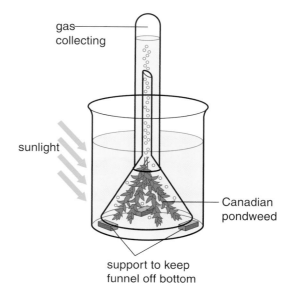

gas collecting

sunlight

Canadian pondweed

support to keep funnel off bottom

a From where does the pondweed get the carbon dioxide that it needs for photosynthesis?

b Suggest how you could investigate how the rate of photosynthesis depends on light intensity.

c State two control variables in this investigation and explain why they need to be controlled.

d Why would an oxygen probe and a datalogger be very useful for this investigation?

e Sketch a graph to show how the rate of photosynthesis depends on light intensity.

9 What is happening when the levels of oxygen and carbon dioxide remain the same near the leaves of a living plant?

10 Oxygen was naturally in the atmosphere when the Earth was formed. However, it did not stay in the atmosphere for long. What happened to it?

11 Explain why oxygen in a planet's atmosphere would suggest that the planet harbours life.

How did I do?

I can write a word equation for photosynthesis.	✔ ☐
I can describe an experiment to demonstrate photosynthesis in variegated leaves.	☐
I can explain why photosynthesis in plants is vital for human life.	☐

Teacher's tips

When you have learnt the basic equation for **respiration**, in words or symbols, you have also learnt the equation for **photosynthesis** as this is the respiration equation in reverse!

35: Leaves and roots

You will revise:
- the tissue structure of leaves and roots
- how these structures help photosynthesis
- transporting chemicals inside the plants.

Get started

The leaves and roots of a plant are both organs that perform specific functions. Leaves are involved in photosynthesis and roots in obtaining water and minerals from the soil (as well as holding the plant in place).

Practice

1. Why do the cells on the top side of leaves have many more chloroplasts than the cells on the bottom?

2. Explain the advantage of leaves having a large surface area.

3. Why are leaves and roots organs rather than tissues or systems?

4. Why do leaves need a large supply of water?

Challenge

5. You can investigate where photosynthesis takes place by using variegated leaves.

    a What is a variegated leaf?

    b Describe how you can show that photosynthesis takes place only in the green sections of the leaf.

6. a The veins in a leaf provide structure to keep the leaf rigid. What is their role in photosynthesis?

    b Little openings called stomata are present on the underside of the leaf. Why are they open during the day and closed during the night?

    c Above the stomata are little air spaces within the leaf. Suggest what these are for.

    d The stomata in the leaves regulate the amount of water loss. Suggest why the upper layer of the leaf has a waxy surface.

    e Why is the distance between the top and the bottom of the leaf usually very small?

7. One product of photosynthesis in a leaf is glucose. As well as for respiration, it has a wide range of uses within the plant.

    a Why is glucose converted into starch?

    b Glucose is often converted into other sugars such as fructose. This makes their fruits nice to eat. What is the advantage of this to the plant?

c Amino acids are formed from glucose combining with other elements such as nitrogen. Where do these other elements come from? Why are amino acids so important?

d Glucose can be turned into a carbohydrate called cellulose. What part of the plant cell is made from this material?

e The cell membranes are made from fats (again, made from glucose). What is the role of the membrane in cell function?

8 Here is a diagram of a root.

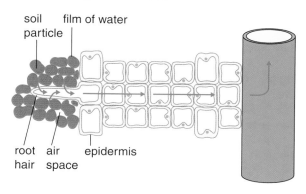

a There are hundreds of root hairs per square centimetre of root. In what way does this help the function of the root?

b Why are there no chloroplasts in the root cells?

c Root cells need to respire. Where do they get their oxygen from?

d Why do plants need minerals as well as water?

e Water enters the cells by diffusion but the minerals need active transport. Suggest which one of these methods requires some of the plant's energy.

9 What is the role of the xylem and the phloem in plant function? How is this role performed in the human body?

10 Some plants in mineral-deficient habitats have developed a different way of obtaining minerals rather than using the soil. What sort of plants are these?

How did I do?

I can draw diagrams of typical leaf and a root cells. ☐

I can explain how the cells are adapted for their particular function. ☐

I can describe the difference in the tissue found on the top of a leaf compared to the bottom of a leaf. ☐

Teacher's tips

It is time well spent familiarising yourself with a diagram of a **transverse section** through a **leaf** as you can revise lots of important structures and processes while doing so. For example, adaptations, gas exchange, respiration, photosynthesis and transport.

36: Metals and acids

Get started

A very large proportion of the elements are metals. Most metals have similar physical properties but this family of elements can also be explored by studying the way they behave chemically. In particular, how do metals react with acids?

Practice

1 Where do metals appear on the periodic table?

2 Which metal is liquid at room temperature? Are any metals gases at this temperature?

3 Which metallic elements are magnetic?

4 Which gaseous element is usually produced when a metal reacts with an acid?

Challenge

5 a How do metals differ in appearance to non-metals (in the solid state)?

b The density of metals tends to be higher than the density of non-metals. Suggest how solid metals and non-metals differ in their structure.

c Metals can be polycrystalline. What does this mean?

d How do metals and non-metals differ in their ability to conduct heat?

e Do all metals conduct electricity equally well? What is special about graphite?

f State one advantage and one disadvantage of using metals as building materials.

6 Some sodium reacts with concentrated hydrochloric acid.

a Why would you be advised not to carry out this experiment in a school laboratory?

b What gas is produced from this reaction and how would you test for it?

c Once all of the sodium has reacted, how could you extract the solute from the solution?

d State the name of the solute that remains.

7 Here are formulae for some well-known chemicals:

Hydrogen gas: H_2
Hydrochloric acid: HCl
Sulfuric acid: H_2SO_4
Zinc sulfate: $ZnSO_4$
Zinc chloride: $ZnCl_2$

    a Write down a balanced symbol equation for the reaction of zinc with

       i sulfuric acid and   **ii** hydrochloric acid.

    b What general name do we give to compounds like zinc sulfate and zinc chloride?

    c Which other chemical is always present in these reactions?

    d Suggest why this chemical plays a very important role in these reactions.

8 **a** What name do we call the compound K_2SO_4?

    b Explain how you could obtain a sample of this substance from the reaction of a metal and an acid.

    c Write down a balanced symbol equation for this reaction.

9 Copy and complete this word equation for the reaction between most metals and acids.

    Metal + acid → . . . . . . + ...

10 CO_2 is called carbon dioxide. Why is $ZnCl_2$ called zinc chloride rather than zinc dichloride?

11 If you add 3 g of sodium to 200 ml of 0.5M sulfuric acid, the theoretical yield of sodium sulfate is 12.6 g.

    a Suggest what is meant by theoretical yield.

    b Explain why the mass of sodium sulfate produced is bigger than the original mass of the sodium.

    c What would the theoretical yield be if you added 2 g of sodium to the same amount of sulfuric acid?

    d Suggest why the theoretical yield is still 12.6 g when you add 5 g of sodium to the acid.

Teacher's tips

It is worth constructing a simple table which summarises the key differences between **metals** and **non-metals** as this is a popular examination question. Table headings should be:

- position in the periodic table
- physical properties
- electrical conductivity
- thermal conductivity
- ability to displace hydrogen from a dilute acid.

37: Reactivity of metals

You will revise:
- the reactivity series of metals
- the reactions of Group I and Group II metals with water
- other experimental methods for determining reactivity.

Get started

Some metals are more reactive than others. By studying chemical reactions we can place metals in a reactivity series. This helps us to predict what is going to happen in certain chemical reactions.

Practice

1 Explain why gold is found as an element in rocks rather than as a compound.

2 What is meant by the tarnishing of metals?

3 Suggest why the Bronze Age occurred before the Iron Age.

4 What chemical compound is rust? How does rust form? Why can it be a problem?

Challenge

5 Gold and sodium are both soft metals. When they are freshly cut, they are both shiny, but sodium quickly becomes dull in appearance. The gold, however, remains shiny.

   a Explain the difference in this behaviour.

   b Why do only the surfaces of metals become tarnished?

6 You have been given some magnesium, iron, copper and zinc and asked to determine their order of reactivity.

To start with, you try placing the different metals in dilute hydrochloric acid. The magnesium reacted quickly, the zinc and the iron reacted quite slowly and the copper didn't react at all.

   a State two variables you need to control in order to make it a fair test.

   b Which two metals can you already place in the reactivity series?

To test the reactivity of the other two metals you decide to collect the gas that they produce.

   c What is the gas produced? How could you test for it?

   d Suggest how you could determine which was the more reactive of these two metals.

7 The first three elements of Group I of the periodic table are lithium, sodium and potassium.

  a What are the chemical symbols for these three elements?

  b Summarise what you see when you place a small piece of each of these metals in water.

  c What gas is given off in these reactions? Why is this dangerous?

  d How could you show that the remaining solution is alkaline?

  e Write down these three elements in order of decreasing reactivity.

  f What are the metals further down this group? Why can't you see the reaction between these metals and water in a school lab?

  g Suggest why these three elements are highly flammable. Explain why it is inadvisable to put out a fire involving these metals with a water extinguisher.

  h Magnesium is a Group II metal that only reacts slowly with water. However, it does react with steam. State whether magnesium is more or less reactive than lithium.

  i Calcium, a Group II metal below magnesium in the periodic table, reacts fairly easily in cold water. Suggest how the reactivity of the Group II metals changes as you go down the group.

8 a What reaction is happening when you heat a metal in air?

  b Write a general equation for this reaction.

  c What does this suggest about the reactivity of the oxygen in the air compared to nitrogen or the noble gases?

  d Suggest what happens when you heat gold in air.

9 Suggest four properties of gold that make it suitable for extraction by 'panning' the sediment from streams. Explain your answer.

10 How can the reactivity series of metals be worked out using salt solutions and a voltmeter?

Teacher's tips

As well as being asked questions about the reactivity series, you could be asked to explain what the reactivity series is, so learn the following definition. The reactivity series is a list of metals displayed in the order of how quickly they react with oxygen, water and acids. The first metal in the list is the most reactive and the last the least. Make up a **mnemonic** to help you remember the order.

38: Acidity in the environment

You will revise:
- what we mean by acid rain
- natural and human causes of acid rain
- the harmful effects of acid rain on the environment.

Get started

Rain is naturally slightly acidic. However, the activity of humans has sometimes increased this acidity, causing damage to the environment.

Practice

1 Carefully define what we mean by acid rain.

2 Explain what is meant by the weathering of rocks.

3 How does weathering lead to the formation of soils?

4 Why do you find many more lichens on trees in the countryside than you do in a city?

Challenge

5 a Carbon dioxide, sulfur dioxide and nitrogen dioxide all dissolve in water to form different types of acid. Write down an acid that is formed from each of these compounds.

b Give an example of the natural production of carbon dioxide.

c Why is the rain particularly acidic following a volcanic eruption?

6 Car exhausts emit nitrogen monoxide which can lead to acid rain. In recent years all new cars have been fitted with catalytic converters. The following reaction occurs inside the converters:

$$2CO + 2NO \rightarrow 2CO_2 + N_2$$

a What other harmful gas does the catalytic converter remove from the exhaust fumes?

b Explain why, even if all of the nitrogen monoxide is removed, car exhausts still lead to acid rain.

c What conclusion can you reach about the acidity of nitric acid and carbonic acid?

7 a What is the difference between erosion and corrosion?

b Why is limestone particularly susceptible to acid rain?

c Explain why acid rain could be particularly damaging in big cities in hot climates.

d Iron railings can gradually get thinner due to the action of acid rain. Would this also happen with gold railings? Explain your answer.

8 **a** Acid rain can dissolve minerals in the soil, which can then flow away with the rainwater. Explain why this is a major problem for plants.

b Acid rain can also directly damage plants. Explain why acidic mist is likely to be even more damaging.

c In Sweden, lakes are sprayed with limestone every few years. How does the limestone reduce the effect of acid rain? Why does the process have to be repeated?

9 Here is a diagram showing a cross-section of some soil.

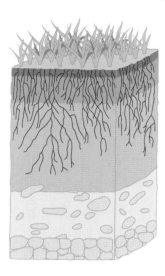

a What is the main cause of the weathering of the rocks at the bottom of the soil?

b Besides the minerals from the rocks, how do the other minerals get into the soil (assuming no human intervention)?

c In Scandinavian countries, the soil is coarse textured, allowing water to move easily. Some base minerals form alkaline solutions in the water. Explain why the soil is often very acidic.

10 Why are scientists investigating the use of limestone-secreting bacteria in preservation work?

11 State and explain three factors that can affect the pH of natural soil.

12 Why is acid rain becoming less of a problem than it was a generation ago?

How did I do?

✔

I can explain how acid rain is produced naturally. ☐

I can discuss how human activities are leading to increased levels of acid rain. ☐

I can describe what effects these increased levels are having on the environment. ☐

Teacher's tips

Once you have a clear appreciation of what acid rain is, what causes it and what its effects on the environment are, you should concentrate on learning the ways in which acid rain can be **reduced** as this is often asked at the end of a question about acid rain. For example, car exhausts are fitted with a catalytic converter and oil refineries remove sulfur during the refining process.

39: Air pollution and global warming

You will revise:

- various ways in which humans are polluting the atmosphere
- greenhouse gases and global warming
- possible impacts of global warming
- ways in which we can reduce air pollution.

Get started

Human life since the Industrial Revolution has become much easier but our activities have caused damage to the environment. Can we solve the problem of air pollution or have we left a legacy for hundreds of years to come?

Practice

1 State a reason why air pollution has become more of a problem in the last few hundred years.

2 What is the difference between global warming and climate change?

3 Why is carbon dioxide called a greenhouse gas?

4 Besides polluting the atmosphere, what is the main problem of using fossil fuels as an energy resource?

Challenge

5 a What chemical element is present in ozone?

   b The ozone layer is high up in the atmosphere and absorbs a lot of ultraviolet light from the Sun. Why is this essential for our survival?

   c Why has the use of chlorofluorocarbons (CFCs) been phased out in recent years?

   d Give one example where CFCs have been used in the past.

   e Why will it take a very long time for this ban to have a sizeable effect on the environment?

6 When the fuel in a car engine doesn't burn efficiently, carbon monoxide is formed.

   a What is the chemical formula for carbon monoxide?

   b Carbon monoxide atoms readily attach themselves to haemoglobin in the blood. Why is carbon monoxide such a dangerous gas?

   c Why can carbon monoxide poisoning due to a faulty gas boiler catch you unawares?

7 What is smog? Why is it less likely to occur in big cities than it did in the 1950s?

8 **a** Explain why most factories and power stations have very tall chimneys.

b Does this ultimately solve the pollution problem?

c When particles of soot pass electrical wires at very high negative voltage they become negatively charged. Explain how the presence of positively charged plates within a chimney can extract the soot from the exhaust gases.

9 **a** What is biodegradable waste?

b Explain why biodegradable waste is less harmful to the environment.

10 **a** Explain how the presence of carbon dioxide (and other greenhouse gases) in the atmosphere leads to the surface of the Earth being hotter than it would have been.

b Did the greenhouse effect happen before humans polluted the atmosphere?

c How do we know that levels of carbon dioxide have risen dramatically since the 1950s?

d Give two reasons why global warming will lead to higher sea levels.

e Researchers can find information about the carbon dioxide content of the atmosphere and the temperature of the climate from millions of years ago by drilling deep into the ice in Antarctica. Why is this data useful in helping us to predict what is going to happen in the future?

f Most scientists agree that the Earth's average temperature rose by 0.6 °C in the 20th century. Why was this measurement very difficult to make?

11 Will the melting of icebergs lead to a rise in sea levels? Do an experiment with an ice cube floating in some water to find out. Try to explain what is going on.

12 State two other factors that might be the reason for global warming other than increased carbon dioxide levels.

13 Some people have suggested that climate change could disrupt the Gulf Stream. What is the Gulf Stream? What impact would it have on the UK climate if it stopped?

14 Scientists have concluded that spring in the UK is getting slightly earlier every year. Why can plants adapt to the changing climate faster than animals? What impact could this have on bird life and animals further up the food chain?

How did I do?

I can explain why there is a hole in the ozone layer and why this is bad news. ✔ ☐

I can describe what we mean by smog and ways in which we can reduce it appearing. ☐

I can discuss the likely impact of increased carbon dioxide emissions on the environment. ☐

Teacher's tips

One of the best things to do with regards to **global warming** is to learn a couple of consequences of the process as these are often tested in examination questions.

Suggestions include:

• a change in global weather patterns resulting in the establishment of drought regions and regions susceptible to flooding
• melting of polar ice caps leading to a rise in sea levels, associated flooding of low-lying land and increased erosion of coastal regions.

40: Energy and electricity

You will revise:
- energy transfers in an electric circuit
- using voltmeters and ammeters to measure voltage and current
- studying energy transfers by measuring the voltage.

Get started

Electric circuits involve energy being transferred from one form to another. You can examine how the energy changes by considering the voltage between various points in the circuit.

Practice

1. What energy happens inside a cell?

2. How do you connect ammeters and voltmeters in a circuit?

3. What is the voltage between two points in a circuit actually a measure of?

4. Explain the difference between an energy transformation and an energy transfer.

Challenge

5. What useful energy transfers happen in the following devices?

   a Electric motor   b Microphone

   c Variable resistor   d Solar cell

6. a Explain the principle of conservation of energy.

   b When we burn fossil fuels, where does the wasted energy go?

7. Here are some diagrams showing how two light bulbs transfer the energy.

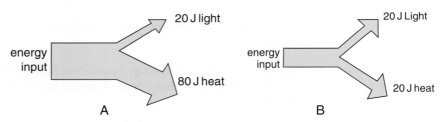

A   B

   a How much energy has each light bulb used?

   b Which light bulb is the most efficient? Explain your answer.

8 This diagram shows a circuit with various places where a voltmeter can be connected.

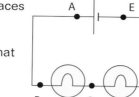

a Explain, in terms of electrical charges, what we mean by a current.

b If the connecting wires behave perfectly, how much electrical energy is transferred into other forms of energy between points A and B?

c What value would a voltmeter display if it was connected to A and B?

d Copy and complete the following table (assume the light bulbs are identical).

Places where voltmeter is connected	Voltmeter reading
A and E	i
B and D	ii
B and C	iii
C and D	iv
D and E	v

e Another identical light bulb is added in series to the circuit. What would the voltmeter read if it was connected across i one light bulb, ii two light bulbs?

9 You can make a cell to power an electrical clock by placing copper and magnesium electrodes in a potato.

a Where does the energy which powers the clock come from?

b Why does the cell run out?

c Explain why the cell wouldn't work if you used two copper electrodes instead.

d Potassium is a more reactive metal than magnesium and would produce a higher voltage. Why would it be difficult to use a potassium electrode?

10 The proper term for voltage is *potential difference*. Explain why this term is used. Assuming each charge carrier has an electrical potential energy of 2 J as it emerges from the positive terminal, how does the energy of the charge carriers vary as they move around the circuit (starting at A) in question **8**?

How did I do?

I can describe the energy transfers occurring in a particular electric circuit. ✔ ☐

I can connect ammeters and voltmeters to measure current and voltage. ☐

I can explain how voltages vary across components in a circuit in terms of energy transformations. ☐

Teacher's tips

Do not get an **ammeter** confused with a **voltmeter**. An ammeter measures the size of the current, in units called amperes, flowing around an electric circuit. A voltmeter measures the difference in electric potential, in units called volts, between any two parts of an electric circuit.

41: Electricity and modern

You will revise:
- why electricity is so useful
- how electricity is produced
- the relationship between energy and power
- calculating electricity costs.

Get started

It is difficult to overestimate the impact that electricity has had on modern life. However, if we are to keep the costs down and have a sustainable future, we must use it efficiently.

Practice

1. State one advantage and one disadvantage of using mains electricity rather than batteries.

2. What is the voltage of mains electricity in houses in the UK?

3. When would you use a 10 W light bulb instead of a 100 W light bulb (assuming they have the same efficiency)?

Challenge

4. a Why do we sometimes call electricity a secondary fuel?

   b By considering the energy transformations in useful devices around the home, explain why electricity is a very useful source of energy.

   c State one other reason why electricity is a useful resource.

5. a The total current entering a house is 60 A. Under normal operating conditions, what value would the current leaving the house be?

   b Why would there be cause for concern if the current leaving the house was at a smaller value than this?

   c Are the mains sockets in buildings connected in series or parallel? Explain your answer.

   d When there is a larger current flowing into the house, the electricity meter 'counts up' at a faster rate. What quantity is it measuring?

6. The amount of electrical energy you use is charged in kilowatt-hours (or units). Here is the formula to work it out:

   energy (in kW h) = power (in kW) × time (in hours).

   a If the electricity company charge 10p per kilowatt-hour, how much does it cost to watch a 0.5 kW TV for 8 hours?

   b How many units are used when a 100 W light bulb is switched on for 20 minutes? (1 kW = 1000 W)

7 A teacher set up the following apparatus

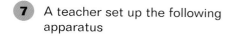

12 V power supply

12 W light bulb

joule-meter

a The joulemeter clicked every time the light bulb transformed 10 J of energy. What energy transfers are taking place?

b What did pupils hear when the teacher adjusted the variable resistor to make the light bulb brighter?

c The teacher took out the 12 W light bulb and replaced it with a 24 W bulb. The variable resistor was not changed. What did the pupils see and hear that was different?

d What is the relationship between power and energy?

e What would happen if the teacher replaced the 24 W bulb with a more efficient bulb of the same brightness?

8 Here is a diagram of a simple dynamo.

a What energy transfers takes place inside the dynamo?

b Why is the coil wound on a piece of iron?

c State three things you could do to make the current larger.

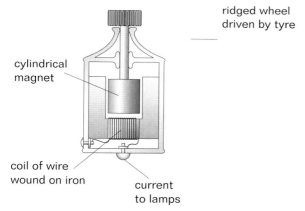

ridged wheel driven by tyre

cylindrical magnet

coil of wire wound on iron

current to lamps

9 Why do electricity companies have to follow the TV schedules very closely?

10 Explain why electricity is transmitted along power lines at such a high voltage. Why don't birds sitting on the lines get an electric shock?

How did I do?

	✔
I can give two reasons why electricity is very useful.	☐
I can state how the power of a light bulb is related to the energy it uses.	☐
I can calculate the electrical energy used in kWh and how much it will cost.	☐

Teacher's tips

Examination papers often have one or more questions that involve numerical calculations. This particular section lends itself to this so make sure you know how to calculate the amount of electrical energy used using the equation:

Energy (kWh) = power (kW) x time (hours)

42: Gravity and orbits

You will revise:
- the difference between mass and weight
- how forces affect motion
- why gravity makes objects orbit more massive objects.

Get started

The force of gravity is an attractive force between all masses. The size of the force depends on the amount of mass and the distance. Gravity can make objects in space orbit more massive objects.

Practice

1 What is the definition of an object's weight?

2 How does this differ from an object's mass?

3 If the Sun's gravity suddenly disappeared, what would be the motion of the Earth?

4 Why do we feel the gravity from the Earth much more than the gravity from the Sun?

Challenge

5 **a** If the Earth pulls with a force of 10 N on every kg mass on its surface. What is the weight of **i** 60 kg, **ii** 500 g?

   b What mass has a weight of **i** 50 N, **ii** 1 N on the Earth?

6 **a** Give one reason why the pull of the Moon's gravity on objects at its surface is one-sixth as much as the Earth's.

   b What is the weight of a 60 kg object on the Moon?

   c What mass has a weight of 12 N on the Moon?

7 A spaceship has a weight of 2400 N on the Moon. It then goes to a planet where it has a weight of 32 000 N.

Find **a** the mass of the spaceship and **b** the force with which gravity pulls on 1 kg of matter on the planet.

8 **a** Which way does the Sun's gravity pull you at noon?

   b If you dug down to the centre of the Earth (and survived), what would you notice about the gravity acting on you?

   c Explain why the Moon orbits the Earth rather than the Sun even though the Sun has a larger mass.

9 **a** A rocket has a weight of 10 000 N. Explain why the rocket motor has to provide a force greater than 10 000 N in order to accelerate the rocket upwards.

    b Once the rocket has taken off its acceleration increases although the rocket motor is providing the same force. Suggest two reasons why the acceleration increases.

    c The rocket reaches deep outer space and the rocket motors are switched off. What is the motion of the rocket now?

10 You are whirling a conker above your head in a horizontal circle.

    a What direction must the force act on the conker to keep it moving in a circle?

    b What would happen to the conker if you let go of the string?

    c When a car goes around a roundabout, what provides the force that makes it go in a circle? What might happen if there is ice on the road?

11 Here is a diagram of the path that a rock would follow if you threw it sideways while standing on a chair.

    a What is making the rock fall to the ground? Which direction does this force act?

    b Why doesn't the rock simply fall vertically?

    c Copy the diagram and include the path the rock would follow if you threw it faster.

    d If you throw the rock at about 7 km/s it falls at the same rate as the Earth curves away. What would the rock do if there are no obstructions (and there was no air resistance)?

    e Why don't objects need to be as fast as this to behave in the same way if they are further away from the Earth?

12 The Earth actually bulges at the equator due to its rotation. How does your weight vary between the equator and the North Pole? Explain your answer.

13 You dig a tunnel downwards to the centre of the Earth and then all the way to the other side of the Earth. You then stand on the surface of the Earth by the opening of the tunnel and jump into the tunnel. What would your motion be?

How did I do?

I can calculate the weight of an object on Earth if I know its mass. ✔ ☐

I can do calculations based on masses and weights of objects if they are on the Moon or other planets. ☐

I can describe the motion of an object if there is an unbalanced force on it. ☐

I can explain how gravity can make objects move in circular orbits. ☐

Teacher's tips

It is absolutely imperative that you appreciate the difference between **mass** and **weight**. Many students use these terms in the wrong context and lose vital marks in examinations – make sure you are not one of them!

- the **mass** of an object is a measure of the amount of **matter** found in that object (remember m's go together: 'mass' goes with 'matter'!)
- the **weight** of an object is the **pull** of the **Earth's gravity** on the object.

43: Understanding the Solar System

Get started

Early models of the Solar System lasted for a very long time before observations and new scientific theories forced people to accept that these models were wrong. In recent years our understanding of the Solar System has quickly improved due to the use of artificial satellites and space probes.

Practice

1 Before the seventeenth century, which object did most people think was at the centre of the Solar System?

2 What invention led to the realisation that the Sun was at the centre of the Solar System?

3 Why did it take many years for most people in western civilisations to accept that this was indeed the case?

4 What is the benefit of having a telescope up in space?

Challenge

5 This question is about artificial satellites.

a What is a geostationary (or geosynchronous) orbit?

b What are satellites in geostationary orbits generally used for? What is the advantage of this particular type of orbit?

c What is a polar orbit?

d Polar orbits are much nearer to the Earth than geostationary orbits. Explain why this means that they must orbit the Earth much more quickly.

e Explain how satellites in polar orbits can photograph most of the Earth's surface over a period of 24 hours.

f State two uses of polar satellites.

g Draw a diagram of the Earth and the orbits of a geostationary and a polar satellite.

h What are satellites orbiting other planets used for?

6 **a** What is the evidence in the night sky that the Earth is spinning?

   b If you didn't know that the Earth was spinning, what other conclusion could you reach about the motion of the stars?

   c To the unaided eye, the visible planets look just like stars. Where does the light from the planets ultimately come from?

   d How did astronomers know that the planets were different to the stars before the telescope was invented?

7 In AD 140 Ptolemy produced a model of the Universe that fitted the known facts of the time.

   a Why was it important that the model fitted the known facts?

   b Astronomers noticed that the planets other than Mercury and Venus spent some of their orbits (around the Earth remember) going backwards. How did Ptolemy adapt his model to account for this motion?

   c As time went on and astronomers made better measurements, the model had to be continually altered. Why was this?

   d In 1543 Copernicus suggested that a model of the Universe with the Sun at its centre fitted the facts just as well and was a lot simpler. Why was he largely ignored?

8 **a** How did Galileo's telescopic observations of Jupiter prove that not everything orbited the Earth?

   b People originally believed that gravity was due to objects trying to get to the centre of the Universe. Why was this 'evidence' for Ptolemy's Earth-centred model?

   c What role did Newton play in leading most people to accept the fact that the Sun was at the centre of the Universe?

9 We now know that the Sun is not at the centre of the Universe. Briefly describe our understanding of the structure of the Universe today.

10 There has been much debate recently about whether Pluto should be called a planet. What discoveries have led to this debate?

11 Newton's theory of gravity led to the discovery of a new planet. How did this come about? Why did this add weight to the evidence that his theory was correct?

12 What sort of object do we think we are orbiting at the centre of the Milky Way galaxy? What is the evidence for this?

How did I do?

I can outline the evidence that led to us realising that the Sun was at the centre of the Solar System rather than the Earth. ✔

I can discuss why these changing ideas met a lot of resistance. ☐

I can draw diagrams of geostationary and polar orbits and explain the uses of satellites that travel in these orbits. ☐

Teacher's tips

Compile a **list** of the **uses of artificial satellites** as questions of require a knowledge of these. For example:

- global communication – television, radio and telephone signals
- weather monitoring – weather forecasts
- observing the Earth – compiling maps.

You will revise:

- the formula linking average speed, distance and time
- converting the units for speed
- calculating speeds, distances and times
- measuring the speed at a point.

Get started

The average speed of a car journey is the distance travelled divided by the time taken. However, the speed often changes, from accelerating up to high speed on a motorway to slowing to a stop at some traffic lights. How can speed be measured more precisely and how can it be measured at a point?

Practice

1. Write down the formula that links average speed, distance and time.

2. A car goes a certain distance in a certain time. If another car goes half the distance in a third of the time, is its average speed faster or slower?

3. How many metres are there in a kilometre? How many seconds are there in an hour?

4. The Earth orbits the Sun at a speed of 30 km/s. What is this speed in km/h?

5. If a jet aeroplane is travelling at 1200 km/h, how far does it travel per second?

Challenge

6. Convert the following speeds into different units:

   a 36 km/h into m/h   d 72 m/s into km/h

   b 36 km/h into m/s   e 144 km/h into m/s

   c 200 m/s into km/s   f 20 m/s into km/h

7. Two bikes are racing down a hill. The first bike is going at a constant speed of 10 m/s and the second bike is gradually accelerating from rest. Both bikes start at the top and arrive at the bottom of the hill together.

   a What is the average speed of the second bike?

   b Which bike was in front at the halfway point?

8. I walk to my friend's house, which is 6 km away. At exactly the moment I leave my house, my friend leaves her house and walks towards me. If I am walking twice as fast as my friend, how far away from my house do we meet?

9 A teacher is timing the winning time of a school 100 m race. After the starting pistol has been fired, he fumbles a little before he manages to start the stopwatch. If the average speed was calculated from this time, would it be too fast or too slow?

10 A teacher sets up an air track with two light gates connected to a datalogger. The card on the 'glider' that breaks the beam of the light gates is 2 cm long. The datalogger is set up to read the times that the beams of light have been broken. When the glider was sent along the air track, the first light gate read a time of 0.102 s and the second light gate read a time of 0.051 s.

   a Was the glider speeding up or slowing down?

   b Calculate the speeds in cm/s at the two light gates.

   c Would it be possible to work out the average speed of the glider from the data you have been given? Explain your answer.

   d Can the light gates give you the actual speed the glider was travelling as it went past them or is this still an average speed?

11 Here is a diagram showing the basic parts of a speedometer in a car.

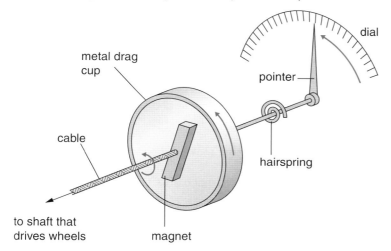

   a As the magnet turns, it exerts a force on the metal drag cup. Explain how the rest of the speedometer works.

   b Does the speedometer measure an average speed or does it measure the speed at a point? Explain your answer.

How did I do?

I can calculate the average speed from the distance and the time. ☐

I can convert speeds between m/s and km/h. ☐

I can analyse different motions and carry out calculations based on them. ☐

I can describe how a speedometer works. ☐

Teacher's tips

The most straightforward way to manipulate speed, distance and time calculations is to construct and use a **formula triangle**.

To calculate distance, speed or time simply cover the value you want to calculate and the remaining two letters tell you how to calculate the value.

For example, to work out time, cover the t and you can see that t can be calculated by distance divided by speed.

45: Forces and motion

You will revise:
- the motion of objects when the forces are balanced or unbalanced
- how the force of air resistance changes with speed
- terminal velocity and why things have a maximum speed.

Get started

When the forces are balanced, an object will maintain its present speed. However, unbalanced forces make the object speed up, slow down or change direction.

Practice

1. The right-hand pedal in a car changes the force provided by the engine. Why is it called an accelerator?

2. How does the maximum acceleration of a car change when it is fully loaded?

3. How does the air feel different when you are riding a bicycle quickly? How do you reduce this effect?

4. What is terminal velocity?

5. Explain the difference between upthrust and air resistance.

Challenge

6. When you stop pedalling on a bicycle and freewheel you will gradually slow down.

   a. What is the main force that makes you slow down to start with?

   b. Why doesn't this force have much effect when you are going slowly?

   c. Explain why you slow down more quickly when you apply the brakes.

   d. Why do you skid if you apply the brakes too quickly?

7. Many car manufacturers give the time it takes for a car to get from 0 to 60 mph.

   a. If a car can get from 0 to 60 mph in 4.8 s is its acceleration more or less than a car that can get from 0 to 60 mph in 10 s?

   b. State and explain three factors that car manufacturers can change in their cars to improve these times.

   c. Why do cars have a maximum speed rather than just being able to accelerate for ever?

   d. Does the mass of a car affect its maximum speed? Explain your answer.

8 Here is a speed–time graph of a scrunched-up piece of paper falling through the air.

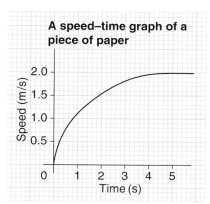

a Describe the motion shown by the graph.

b State the two forces acting on the piece of paper and the direction they are acting in.

c How does the size of each of these forces depend on the speed of the paper?

d As the paper gets faster, why does the resultant force downwards get less?

e What happens to the forces when the paper reaches its terminal velocity?

f How many seconds into the journey did the paper reach its terminal velocity? What is the value of this velocity?

g How would the shape of the graph differ if **i** the paper was shaped into a parachute, **ii** the paper was shaped into a dart that pointed vertically downwards?

9 a A space capsule slows down as it enters the atmosphere. What does this mean about the size of the air resistance compared to the capsule's weight?

b What happens to the sizes of the forces as the capsule slows down? Why does it reach a terminal velocity?

c What piece of equipment can the capsule use to reduce its terminal velocity to a safe level for touchdown?

d Why couldn't this equipment be used as the capsule first entered the atmosphere?

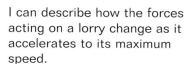

I can state how the size of air resistance depends on the speed that objects move through air. ✔

I can describe how the forces acting on a lorry change as it accelerates to its maximum speed.

I can explain why falling objects reach a terminal velocity.

Teacher's tips

Make sure you can interpret **speed time graphs**.

- A line with a **positive gradient** represents an object whose **speed** is **increasing**
- A line with a **negative gradient** represents an object whose **speed** is **decreasing**
- A **horizontal line**, with no gradient, represents an object whose speed of movement is **constant**.

46: Pressure

You will revise:
- calculating pressures
- pressures in gases
- using hydraulic machines.

Get started

The pressure produced by a force depends on the area of the surface the force is acting on. By understanding pressure, we can design machines to make our lives easier.

Practice

1 Write down the formula relating pressure, force and surface area.

2 The force has to be perpendicular to the surface area. What does perpendicular mean?

3 Why do your ears hurt more and more when you dive deeper into water?

4 What is the difference between a hydraulic and a pneumatic system?

Challenge

5 A 1 kg rectangular block (with weight 10 N) measuring 2 cm by 1 cm by 4 cm is placed on a table.

  a What is the largest pressure the block can exert on the table?

  b What is the least pressure?

6 Give an example in nature where an animal's body has been designed to produce as much pressure as possible and another example where part of the body has been designed to produce as little pressure as possible.

7 Here is a simple hydraulic jack.

  a Why wouldn't the jack work very well using air instead of liquid?

  b What pressure is in the liquid?

  c What load is the 2 N force managing to lift?

  d By how much does the jack multiply the forces?

force = 2 N   load   area = 0.05 m²   area = 2 m²   water

8 To make sure that a vehicle is safe, you need to check the air pressure in the tyres.

    a Why are pressures that are too high or low, unsafe?

    b Explain why lorries have four (or more) wheels parallel to each other on a given axle, rather than just two wheels like a car.

    c When roads are covered in snow, why does it sometimes help to let down your tyres?

    d Tractor wheels have a very large radius and their tyres are very wide. Explain why this is useful.

9 The diagram below shows air in a gas syringe and air in a fixed container. The air is then heated.

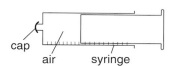

    a In which piece of apparatus will the volume change and the pressure stay the same?

    b What happens to the pressure and volume in the other piece of apparatus?

10 This diagram is of a water-filled balloon pierced with holes. State two pieces of information about the pressure in liquids you can work out from the diagram.

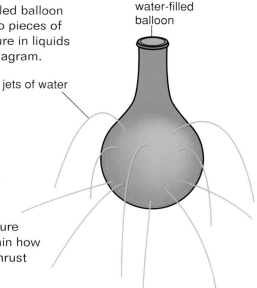
water-filled balloon

jets of water

11 **a** If something is fully submerged in some water (but not touching the bottom), which direction does the water pressure act on
    i the bottom, **ii** the top of the object?

    b By considering how pressure changes with depth, explain how fluids can produce an upthrust force.

How did I do?

I can work out the pressure produced by a force acting on a particular surface. ☐ ✔

I can describe how the pressure in a gas can be increased if its volume remains the same. ☐

I can draw a diagram of a simple hydraulic machine and do simple calculations of forces and pressures to show how it works. ☐

Teacher's tips

Remember the **formula triangle** and how easy it makes calculating unknown values in a set of three? You can also use it to calculate pressure, force and area.

For example, to work out force, cover the f and you can see that force is found by multiplying pressure by area.

Answers

1: Cells

1 The first microscopes were made in 1590 but weren't very good. In 1665 Robert Hooke used a much improved microscope to study the structure of cork. He noticed that there was a regular structure of tiny 'holes' and he called them cells.

2 Cell wall, vacuole, chloroplasts.

3 Nucleus, cytoplasm, cell membrane.

4 They have a large surface area.

5 They are hair-like structures on some cells. They waft things along.

6 So that information can be sent from the central nervous system to muscles a long distance away.

7 a i Nucleus; ii cytoplasm; iii chloroplast; iv vacuole; v cell membrane; vi cell wall.

  b It is a plant cell.

8 a Nucleus.

  b Controls the passage of chemicals in and out of the cell.

  c Cytoplasm.

  d Protects the cell and makes it rigid.

9 An ostrich egg.

10 Animals have skeletons or hard outer shells to keep them rigid; plants don't.

11 The vacuole expands and presses against the outer edge of the cell.

12 The structures in the cell then have a much greater contrast against the cytoplasm.

13 a Diagram A is a root cell; diagram B is a leaf (palisade) cell.

  b Roots are underground – they don't photosynthesise; leaves do photosynthesise and therefore need chloroplasts.

  c To give a large surface area so roots can absorb minerals and water.

  d To protect it on its journey from one plant to another.

14 a B.

  b It has a large surface area to absorb and release chemicals.

  c It helps the sperm to swim towards the egg.

  d To nourish the fertilised egg until the new organism can start feeding.

15 A, B, D, C.

16 Nerve cells. They are very thin so you can't see them unless they are magnified.

17 No. Viruses aren't alive; they are just a collection of genetic material.

2: Reproduction

1 Cells from males and females that fuse together to produce a new organism.

2 a Pollen (male), egg (female).

  b Sperm (male), egg (female).

3 There is a far smaller chance that any single egg gets fertilised and survives. Therefore many more eggs are needed to produce a reasonable number of offspring.

4 Mammals look after their offspring more carefully than other animals (e.g. internal development before birth and producing milk). Therefore there is a greater chance of an offspring's survival and so fewer offspring are needed to keep a viable population.

5 a The main similarity is that two cells fuse together to form a new cell. An amoeba simply splits into two.

  b Flowers contain both female and male sex cells. Sometimes the male sex cell (pollen) fertilises the egg of the same plant. Most animals don't possess both female and male sex cells (they are either male or female) and so this process is impossible.

  c So that the plant's offspring use different resources to their parent. Many animals keep their offspring close so that they can look after and protect them.

6 a The male swims over the eggs and releases sperm into the sea.

b Many eggs don't get fertilised; other species use internal fertilisation. The fertilised eggs are eaten before they hatch and swim away; other species make nests to protect their eggs, or their babies develop inside their bodies.

c The eggs are protected and are less likely to be eaten. There is a greater chance that they will survive and hatch.

d Cod might be eaten by other animals (e.g. humans) or might die of natural causes (due to illness, lack of food, etc.).

e Hardly any energy is used by the cod in looking after their offspring.

7 a i Oviduct, tube which carries the egg from the ovary to the uterus; ii ovary, organ for storing and releasing eggs; iii uterus, organ in which the fetus grows; iv cervix, neck of the uterus; v vagina, has muscular walls to aid childbirth.

b It is a group of organs that work together.

c For example:

i lining of oviduct, wall of uterus;
ii uterus, ovary.

d In the oviduct.

e Identical: one sperm fertilises one egg; this fertilised egg splits into two. Non-identical: two eggs are released into the oviduct and each one is fertilised by a different sperm cell.

f The mammary glands provide food for the young via milk; this contains all the nutrients that a baby needs together with antibodies to fight diseases.

8 a Some inherited characteristics come from the mother.

b A miniature person would contain a miniature person who would contain another miniature person and so on, like Russian dolls. Therefore each man contains an infinite number of miniature people. This is clearly impossible!

9 A hereditary characteristic is a characteristic that has the potential to be passed from parent to offspring. An inherited characteristic is a hereditary characteristic that has actually been passed on from parent to offspring.

10 Mitochondria are very small structures inside cells that provide the cell with energy. Sperm cells need a lot of energy for their journey to reach the egg.

11 Viruses can't reproduce by themselves (they infect cells, which then reproduce the virus). However, bacteria can reproduce by themselves.

12 Asexual reproduction creates clones with exactly the same genetic make-up. Sexual reproduction combines genetic material from the two sex cells; this leads to much greater variety within a species and therefore increases the chances of a population's survival in changing habitats.

3: Habitats, food chains and food webs

1 Nutrients such as food and water; favourable environmental conditions such as light, warmth and shelter.

2 The resources that the habitat provides change during the day.

3 Animals have enough time to prepare for the winter. There is lots of food available from plants.

4 Their food resources are thinly spread.

5 a Organisms that get their energy directly from the Sun.

b Organisms that eat producers.

c Organisms that eat primary consumers.

6 Producers are always plants.

7 A food chain doesn't have any branches; a food web is a collection of food chains.

8 The direction that the energy goes.

9 a Damage to an organism due to the climate.

b Cold temperature; lack of food.

c i Hedgehog; ii swallow. Hibernation: preserves energy when there is a lack of food, but vulnerable to attack from predators. Migration: favourable habitat all year, but requires a lot of energy during the migration.

d Insulates them against the cold; white for camouflage.

e In an inactive state (such as asleep). Deciduous trees shed their leaves in winter and are dormant.

f So that they can take advantage of the light passing through the dormant trees.

10 a The high tide.

b Do an experiment in the lab to see how well they grow but control one of the variables (e.g. keep the salinity the same but vary the dampness, then keep the dampness the same but vary the salinity).

11 a They can 'see' warm-blooded mammals at night time.

b It can kill and eat its prey.

c It has a wide range of vision and spots predators more easily.

d It has very good forward vision – its prey.

e They aren't seen by their prospective quarry or foe.

f This warns predators that they're dangerous.

g They can use many eyes to keep a look-out for predators.

12 a Plant roots → vole → fox; plant roots → vole → owl; bark → woodlice → shrew → owl; bark → woodlice → robin → sparrowhawk; leaves → caterpillar → robin → sparrowhawk; seeds → beetle → fox; seeds → beetle → robin → sparrowhawk; seeds → finch → sparrowhawk.

b They would also decrease due to lack of food.

c Due to a decrease in the robin population, sparrowhawks are more likely to eat the finches.

 4: Variation

1 A feature of appearance or behaviour that is passed on from parent to child via genetic material.

2 The rate of growth is determined by environmental conditions such as light intensity and nutrient supply.

3 The genetic make-up of individuals must be close enough so that the species can reproduce successfully.

4 A Inherited (determined by genetic make-up);

B environment (babies learn to speak the language that is spoken in their immediate surroundings);

C both (people are naturally confident or shy but events in their life can also affect this characteristic);

D inherited (unique to an individual, doesn't change with the environment);

E both (natural IQ but could have a good teacher);

F inherited (determined by genetic make-up);

G both (people are naturally short or tall but nutrition can have a marked affect);

H both (you can lose limbs due to the environment or due to some congenital defect);

I mostly inherited (all humans are born with an ability to learn to speak unless there is a congenital defect or environmental problems in the womb leading to brain damage);

J inherited (determined by genetic make-up);

K environmental (a learnt behaviour).

5 a It might be an inherited characteristic.

b All of the samples have the same genes so any variation will be due to the environment.

6 a They are both continuous variables since they can (theoretically) have any numerical value.

b It means that as the height increases, the weight tends to increase as well.

c The samples were taken from two year groups either side of a growth spurt.

d Not strictly true since one person can be taller than another person but also lighter. However, this statement is true for the general trend.

e They would be tall and thin.

f They might have inherited this characteristic from their parents or it might be due to environmental conditions.

7 a The major cause must be genetic.

b Identical twins share the same genetic make-up. Therefore any variation between them must be down to their environment.

8 It is down to the environment – the temperature of egg incubation.

9 Feral children are children who grow up with no human contact. Their environment is so different to normal that it is much easier to spot which characteristics are adversely affected.

10 This is due to human influence. These groups emerge through selective breeding.

5: Classifying living things

1 A key enables us to efficiently identify what type of specimen we are studying.

2 Plant and animal.

3 Into vertebrates and invertebrates (in the simplified system studied at this level).

4 a A species contains individuals that can reproduce with each other to produce fertile offspring.

b The names are in Latin so that scientists who speak different languages can communicate with each other effectively.

c It would go in front since the *Panthera* group is a subgroup of the mammals and *leo* is a subgroup of *Panthera*.

5 A: invertebrates; B, C, D and E: birds, fish, mammals, reptiles (any order); F: crustaceans; G insects.

6 a Three-sectional bodies, and three pairs of legs.

b Jointed legs and hard outer skeleton.

c It doesn't have a backbone.

d It cannot make its own food.

7 Fish: live only in water. Amphibians: have smooth moist skin, live both on land and in water. Reptiles: have dry scaly skin. Birds: have feathers and wings. Mammals: produce milk to feed young.

8 a Newly discovered species didn't fit into the classification system, so the system had to be adapted to cope with the greater variation.

b It has features common to birds and mammals.

9 Kingdom: Animalia; phylum: Chordata; order: Carnivora; family: Felidae.

10 a More and more newly discovered species didn't fit into the current classification system.

b Humans (kingdom to subspecies): Animalia, Chordata, Vertebrata, Gnathostomata, Osteichthyes, Tetrapoda, Mammalia, Eutheria, Primates, Hominoidea, Hominidae, Homininae, *Homo, sapiens, sapiens*.

11 The original distinguishing feature of mammals is the possession of mammary glands. Duck-billed platypuses have mammary glands (and also share many other characteristics with other mammals).

12 It is not based on physical characteristics but on genetic make-up, which can be investigated by comparing the DNA of different species. It wasn't done in the first place, because the classification system was developed before the theory of evolution and the discovery of DNA.

6: Acids and alkalis

1 A corrosive substance wears away and destroys other material. A caustic substance specifically corrodes organic material (such as human flesh).

2 An alkali is a base that can be dissolved in water.

3 Red in acid, blue in alkali.

4 7.

5 Universal indicator has a different colour for each pH value; litmus paper doesn't.

6 a A Corrosive/caustic; B harmful or irritant; C highly flammable.

   b Wear safety spectacles, wear gloves.

   c It is much easier for them to get inside your body (via breathing).

   d So that, if there is a crash, emergency workers can deal with any spillages safely.

7 a The reaction releases a lot of heat.

   b The acid starts off being very dilute and gradually gets more concentrated instead of the other way round. Therefore much less heat is released to start with.

8 a A bee sting is acid; a wasp sting is alkali.

   b Bee sting: orange/red; wasp sting: blue/purple.

   c It must lie between a pH of 2 and a pH of 10.

   d Wasp sting: use vinegar; bee sting: use baking powder.

9 a A colourless; B yellow; C green.

   b Green to yellow to red.

   c i Red; ii orange (due to B being red and C being yellow); iii yellow; iv blue; v purple (due to A and C being red and B being blue).

   d So that many different pHs can be measured with the same indicator solution.

7: Chemical reactions and burning

1 A chemical change produces a new material, whereas a physical change doesn't.

2 a Reactants.

   b Products.

3 Combustion.

4 Burning is a reaction with oxygen. With a more concentrated reactant, the reaction can happen faster.

5 Exploding is a very sudden expansion rather than a reaction with oxygen.

6 a Carbon and oxygen.

   b It stands for oxygen.

   c It comes from water, which is hydrogen and oxygen.

7 Limewater is calcium hydroxide. This reacts with carbon dioxide: carbon dioxide + calcium hydroxide → calcium carbonate + water. Calcium carbonate is insoluble in water and therefore the solution goes milky.

8 Magnesium + oxygen → magnesium oxide.

9 It starves the reaction of any more air and hence there is no more oxygen available for the reaction.

10 a Methane + oxygen → water + carbon dioxide.

   b Carbon dioxide; it is a greenhouse gas and so contributes to global warming.

11 a Two possible reasons: there was not enough oxygen left, or the CO_2 produced acted as a kind of fire blanket.

   b The volume of the gases in the beaker decreases when the candle burns.

   c The candle would go out quicker because of the smaller percentage of oxygen.

1 The particles couldn't be seen directly, so there was only indirect evidence for this model.

2 Gases and liquids.

3 Solids: particles touching each other in a regular pattern. Liquids: about two-thirds touching each other; particles randomly arranged with lots of gaps throughout. Gases: particles far apart from each other and randomly arranged.

4 a Stays fixed.

   b Can't flow.

   c Becomes shape of container.

   d Stays fixed.

   e Can flow.

   f Can't really be compressed.

   g Becomes volume of container.

   h Can flow.

   i Can easily be compressed.

5 a The particles in a solid are rigidly held together by chemical bonds.

   b Particles can flow past each other easily so the liquid can assume any shape. However, the particles are still bonded together and so the volume can't easily change.

   c The particles are completely free from each other.

   d There are large gaps between the particles in gases but not in liquids and solids.

   e Again, this is due to the large gaps between the particles.

   f The particles are squashed close enough together so they are arranged in the same way as a liquid.

6 Solid: particles vibrate about a fixed position. Liquid: particles move in random directions and can slide past each other. Gas: particles move in random directions and collide with each other.

7 a The particles of gold are heavier than the particles of copper. They are packed closer together.

   b The particles are closer together in water and so, for a given volume of water, there are more particles than in a given volume of steam.

   c Their size doesn't change; it is the distance between them that gets bigger.

8 a Most metals (tungsten freezes at 3400 °C).

   b Most gases (helium boils at −269 °C).

   c You need to break the bonds.

9 a Melting.

   b 0 °C.

   c Broken.

   d 100 °C.

   e Needed.

   f Condensing.

   g Made.

   h Given out.

   i Freezing.

   j 0 °C.

10 They only stop moving at a theoretical temperature called absolute zero (−273 °C). It is impossible to achieve this low temperature in practice.

11 The fourth state of matter is called a plasma. You need to think of the particles (the atoms) containing other particles within them (electrons and nuclei). In the plasma state, the electrons in the atoms are separated from the nuclei.

12 Both involve converting a liquid into a gas. Boiling only happens at one temperature. Boiling occurs in the body of the liquid but evaporation only happens at the surface. Evaporation reduces the temperature of the liquid and its surroundings (which is why evaporation of sweat has a cooling effect).

13 In diamond, all of the carbon atoms are held very strongly together in a tetrahedral structure. In graphite, the carbon atoms link to form layers that are very strongly bonded together but the layers can slide past each other easily. Hence graphite can act as a lubricant.

9: Solutions

1 A solute dissolves in a solvent to form a solution.

2 No, it is simply a physical mixing process. The particles of the solute need to be small enough to fit between the gaps of the solvent particles. This does not happen in a suspension.

3 The solute particles need to be extremely small in the first place to dissolve properly. Therefore they will easily pass through filter paper.

4 Evaporation is the change of state from liquid to gas at the surface of a liquid. Condensation is the change of state from a gas to a liquid.

5 The alcoholic solvent evaporates very easily. Hence the vapour has a greater relative concentration of alcohol than the remaining liquid. Condensing this vapour produces a stronger drink.

6 The total mass before a process is the same as the total mass after it. Mass of solution = mass of solute + mass of solvent.

7 a A saturated solution is one in which no more solute can be dissolved. All of the gaps between the particles have become completely filled.

b Solubility is the maximum mass of solute (in g) that can be dissolved in 100 g of solvent.

c 150 g is 1.5 times as much as 100 g, so you can dissolve 1.5 × 35 = 52.5 g.

8 a Distillation.

b The solvent.

c The solvent particles evaporate more easily than the solute particles. Therefore they leave the solution, leaving the solute particles behind. Condensing the vapour returns the solvent to its liquid state.

9 a The salt can separate into small enough particles to dissolve in the water, but the grit can't. Therefore the salt particles pass through the holes in the filter paper but the grit particles don't. The water particles can evaporate at the temperature of the warm oven but the salt particles can't. Therefore the water particles leave the salt particles behind, which re-crystallise into a solid state.

b More salt can dissolve in the warm water.

c Grind it into small pieces.

d (Mass of pure salt ÷ mass of rock salt) × 100.

e The pupil with the largest percentage of pure salt.

10 a Dyes B and D; the others contain substances not present in the ink sample.

b Particles of the solutes can 'hold on' to the solution particles to varying degrees. As the solvent particles move along the chromatogram, they take the solute particles with them until the solutes 'fall off' in places determined by how strongly they were 'holding on'.

11 Fractional distillation is the process of separating mixtures of liquids by evaporating the solution and condensing it at different temperatures.

10: Energy transfer

1 We are using them up much more quickly than they are being produced.

2 Renewable resources will not run out, non-renewable resources will eventually run out.

3 Biofuel (or biomass).

4 Joules and calories.

5 a Chemical energy. The Sun.

b Fossil fuels are much more concentrated because the organisms have been compressed together.

c Electricity is a secondary fuel because it provides energy but it is produced from other fuels.

d Producing materials such as medicines, plastics and paints; providing fuel for transport.

e Advantages: cheap technology; always available (compared to solar and wind, for example). Disadvantages: fuels are running out and are useful for other things; pollution, particularly carbon dioxide (greenhouse gas) and sulfur dioxide (causes acid rain).

6 a The energy doesn't have to be converted to other forms first.

b Black is a good absorber of solar radiation and silver is a good reflector. Solar panels need to absorb the energy, but the cookers reflect it onto a point where the food is cooked.

c To collect as much energy as possible in a given time.

d Sunny days are few and far between!

e They are the best option since it is much more difficult to get other types of fuel.

7 When they are all aligned – this produces the spring tides.

8 a It ends up as energy used (and wasted as heat) while the organism is living.

b Energy in food is much more concentrated.

9 a 1000 m.

b The man uses energy for other things (such as keeping his body warm) rather than just climbing.

10 a Independent variable: type of food; dependent variable: temperature change.

b Amount of water (fill up to the same mark each time); amount of food (measure out the same mass each time); distance between food and water (measure with a ruler and always use the same distance).

c So that any changes are due only to changes in the independent variable.

d A bar chart.

e $4200 \times$ volume of water (in litres) $\times$ temperature change (in °C).

f A lot of heat energy would escape into the surroundings rather than heating up the water.

11 It is the only energy resource that can be directly used by cells. All other energy resources have to be converted to glucose first.

12 It is converted into glycogen and stored in the liver and the muscles. Excess energy is converted to fat which is also stored in the liver and under the skin.

11: Electric current

1 Series circuits are one complete loop but parallel circuits have branches.

2 The ability to impede the flow of electric current.

3 An ammeter.

4 The ampere (A).

5 A battery is a collection of cells connected together.

6 a One wire connects to the side and one to the 'blob' at the bottom.

b Series circuit with light bulb, switch and cell in one loop.

c From the positive terminal of the cell, round the loop and back into the negative terminal.

d No, it doesn't matter; a switch will break the circuit wherever it is placed in the loop.

e Use a battery of higher voltage (or more cells).

f There is a parabolic (curved) mirror behind the bulb and a lens in front of it.

7 a i D; ii B; iii D; iv D; v none (current is never used up).

b A and C.

c Chemical energy from the cell is converted to electrical energy; a third of this electrical energy is converted into light and heat in each bulb.

8 A1: 0.5 A; A2: 1 A; A3: 0.5 A.

9 a An analogue meter uses a needle and a pointer; a digital meter displays the value as numbers on a screen.

   b A digital ammeter is easier to read (just copy the numbers down) but an analogue meter can be more precise because you can interpolate between the readings (the arrow points between values).

10 Electrons flow in the opposite direction to current. This was discovered after the theory of electric circuits had been developed.

12: Forces and stretching

1 A push or a pull.

2 The newton (N).

3 Use a forcemeter (can be called a newton meter or a spring balance).

4 Weight is a force.

5 The upthrust is the same size as the weight.

6 a Wear safety spectacles; keep your feet away from directly below the experiment.

   b Support a vertical ruler by the experiment. Measure the original length of the band before the experiment. The extension will equal the total length of the band minus the original length.

   c To check that your readings are reliable and to reduce the experimental error.

   d An anomalous point is one that is so far from the line of best fit that you can't put it down to experimental error; it is likely to be a wrong measurement.

   e Stiff regions are at the top and the bottom; a large increase in force results in a small increase in extension.

   f The relationship between force and extension for elastic bands is non-linear; the points on the scale of the forcemeter won't be equally spaced.

7 Vertical arrows of equal length, one pointing up, one pointing down.

8 Useful: friction between brake blocks and wheels, friction between tyres and road (grip helps cycle accelerate); nuisance: air resistance (rider can bend forward and low to become more streamlined), friction in the wheel bearings (use ball bearings and lubricant).

9 Ice skates put more pressure onto the ice which makes it melt. You therefore have a lubricating layer of water beneath the skates.

10 a Mass is the amount of matter (in kg); weight is the force of gravity on it (in N).

   b Mass stays the same; weight gets less (and is zero in deep outer space).

   c No; the scales are affected by your weight although they are calibrated to read your mass.

   d 20 N.

   e 2 kg.

11 a The upthrust reduces the resultant force.

   b 1.5 N.

   c The upthrust would still be 1.5 N when the object is immersed; this is bigger than the weight, so the object will float.

13: The Solar System

1 The times of their sunrise and sunset differ.

2 A solar eclipse is when the Moon blocks out the sunlight; a lunar eclipse is when Earth blocks the moonlight.

3 The stars appear to rotate gradually around the Pole Star since the Earth is spinning.

4 The stars are the only luminous source; the others reflect the Sun's light.

5 Mercury, Venus, Earth, Mars, Jupiter, Saturn, Uranus, Neptune, (Pluto).

6 Venus; it has a reflective atmosphere, is reasonably large and is close to the Sun.

7 The Sun and all the objects that orbit the Sun; objects include planets, asteroids and comets.

8 a

1   2 and 8   3 and 7   4 and 6   5

  b Sunlight reflected from the Earth.

9 a Due south.

  b This is due to the tilt of the Earth's axis; when the hemisphere tilts towards the Sun, the Sun will appear higher in the sky.

  c The summer and winter solstice respectively.

  d You get the longest and the shortest days.

  e The Sun's rays are shining head-on rather than at an angle.

10 a Summer.

  b A: anywhere in the northern hemisphere; B: close to the South Pole; C: anywhere on the equator.

  c The temperature continues to build up because the days continue to be longer then the nights, so the Earth receives more energy than it radiates away.

11 a Gravity.

  b Planets orbit the Sun; satellites orbit the planets.

  c They have further to travel and they travel more slowly.

  d Between the orbits of Mars and Jupiter.

  e A meteorite.

  f The meteorites tend to burn up in the Earth's atmosphere; also craters disappear from the surface due to weathering and plate tectonics.

12 a You need intelligence to design radio transmitters.

  b Artificial radio signals won't be random.

  c It would take a very long time (at least 100 years) for the radio waves to pass between the two.

13 a A planet moves through the sky relative to the stars.

  b An apparent pattern of stars in the sky; stars move relative to each other.

  c It might be brighter (due to its size) or it might be closer.

14: Food

1 Proteins, carbohydrates, fats, vitamins, minerals.

2 Proteins: growth and repair; carbohydrates: energy and fibres for preventing constipation; fats: energy and cell membranes; vitamins: many uses, including seeing, nerve function, digestion of calcium; minerals: many uses, including calcium for bones, iron for haemoglobin.

3 It is a diet in which the body gets the nutrients it needs in the right amounts.

4 People have different lifestyles and different metabolisms.

5 a 35 kg.

  b i Water is used in sweat. **ii** Water is a solvent and allows dissolved chemicals to move around the body with the plasma in the bloodstream.

  c Unlike water, the body stores reserves of food and can begin to digest them if things get really bad.

6 a Carbon and hydrogen.

  b The molecules have varying numbers of carbon, oxygen and hydrogen atoms within them.

  c Fibre: cereals; starch: potatoes; sugar: chocolates.

  d Fibre makes the digested food more solid, helping the muscles in the gut to push the food along.

  e They provide the body with energy.

7 a Proteins are long chains of amino acids.

b Building structures such as muscles; forming enzymes to aid digestion.

c For example, meats, dairy products, fish, pulses.

d Meats and dairy products provide most of the protein in non-vegetarian diets.

8 a Add iodine solution.

b Sugar.

c Biuret test: add food to water, then add sodium hydroxide and copper sulfate solutions.

d Fat.

9 a A is chicken, B is pasta.

b They don't provide enough of the other nutrient groups.

c Type A: pregnant woman or growing child who needs a lot of protein for growth; type B: athlete who needs a lot of carbohydrate for energy.

10 a Very pale and devoid of energy (iron).

b Bandy legs in children and soft bones (vitamin D).

c Nerves stop working properly leading to weak muscles (vitamin B1).

d Bleeding of gums and under the skin (vitamin C).

15: Digestion

1 To break large insoluble molecules into smaller, soluble ones.

2 Food is physically broken up into smaller pieces. The amylase enzyme starts to break down carbohydrates. Mucin in the saliva coats the food to make it easier to swallow.

3 They are called enzymes and they are made from proteins.

4 The enzyme pepsin, which breaks down protein, needs acidic conditions to work properly.

5 a Biting into softer foods.

b Ripping apart tougher foods.

c Grinding foods.

6 a i Oesophagus; **ii** stomach; **iii** liver; **iv** gall bladder; **v** pancreas; **vi** small intestine; **vii** large intestine.

b It is a collection of organs working together to perform a general task.

c liver, gall bladder and pancreas.

d They secrete digestive juices containing enzymes.

7 a It produces pepsin.

b It produces hydrochloric acid.

c Muscles contract in waves along the walls, allowing food to thoroughly mix with digestive juices.

d It stops the stomach digesting itself.

8 a They neutralise the food from the stomach, allowing the other digesting enzymes to work.

b It makes enzymes to aid digestion; it absorbs digested food through its walls.

c They dramatically increase the surface area making digestion much more efficient.

9 a It absorbs water and dissolved vitamins from the food, forming faeces.

b Bacteria and fibre.

c So that the products of digestion can enter the bloodstream easily.

10 a Amylase.

b Pepsin.

c Stomach.

d Fat.

11 a Peristalsis is a series of waves of contraction of muscles passing food along the digestive system.

b The movement of food doesn't rely on gravity.

12 The liver processes the digested food; for example, it converts excess sugars into glycogen.

13 Bile is alkaline, so it neutralises the environment in the small intestine. It emulsifies (breaks up into small globules of liquid) fats to provide a larger surface area for the enzymes to work on.

14 Glucose is absorbed by the small intestine wall and so must go through the capillaries into the veins. Then it goes from the veins to the heart to the lungs, back to the heart, then to cells via arteries and capillaries.

16: Respiration

1 Glucose + oxygen → carbon dioxide + water (+ energy).

2 They are both reactions with oxygen and both produce energy.

3 Haemoglobin in the red blood cells transports oxygen; the plasma carries the others.

4 a Carbon dioxide.

   b The right-hand tube of limewater goes milky.

   c The left-hand tube stays clear. Since the air you breathe in bubbles through this tube, this must mean that it contains less carbon dioxide.

5 a Mammals are warm blooded; they need a lot more energy to maintain their body temperatures.

   b Some plants and animals can respire and photosynthesise underwater.

6 Breathing is used to provide oxygen and to remove carbon dioxide and water vapour. The bloodstream is used to transport oxygen (and glucose) to the cells and carbon dioxide and water to the lungs.

7 Blood comes out of left ventricle and goes through the body; blood from the body enters the right atrium; blood from right ventricle goes through the lungs and then returns to the left atrium.

8 Oxygen can easily attach and detach itself from haemoglobin. Therefore it can be actively transported and delivered to where it is needed.

9 The pulmonary vein carries oxygenated blood from the lungs to the heart.

10 The kidneys filter the blood, keeping the various chemicals in the blood at normal levels.

17: Micro-organisms and disease

1 It is a very tiny organism that can't be seen by the unaided eye.

2 Bacteria can reproduce by themselves; viruses need the help of infected cells.

3 A pathogen.

4 Vectors are animals that carry pathogens from one diseased organism to another.

5 a The instruments aren't carrying any micro-organisms.

   b Gamma radiation.

   c Heat them strongly.

   d To make sure that the micro-organisms you find are due to the experiment you are doing and weren't there anyway.

   e To make sure that your micro-organism colony doesn't cause any diseases.

6 a Bacteria can be seen through an optical microscope. To see viruses you need an electron microscope.

   b Viruses need living cells to reproduce.

   c A protein coat and genetic material.

7 Bacteria don't reproduce as quickly at cold temperatures. Hence the rate of decomposition of the food and the release of toxins is slower.

8 a The skin.

   b It kills many bacteria by disrupting their cell walls.

   c The orifices (entrances) of the body and through open wounds.

d Mucus traps micro-organisms in the mouth and nose.

e These cells waft the mucus up to the mouth. The mucus is then swallowed, passing the bacteria into the digestive system where they are destroyed or excreted.

f They form blood clots which quickly close up open wounds before the skin can repair itself.

9 a Fleming noticed that the bacteria colony didn't grow near some mould that had accidentally landed on the agar jelly.

b There are regions around the antibiotic where no bacteria have survived.

c The one with the largest region where no bacteria have colonised.

d There is no antibiotic that will kill all types of bacteria.

e Bacteria can reproduce very quickly; you need to make sure that you have killed all of them before you finish the antibiotic or the colony will grow again and re-infect.

18: Investigating habitats

1 Sampling is taking data from random places within the habitat. The population size is often too hard to count completely and so you have to take small samples and extrapolate the data to the whole habitat.

2 Take quadrat readings along a straight line, recording all of the organisms you find. A transect is used to study how a habitat changes because of a gradual change in physical conditions – for example, across a path passing through a wood.

3 It is a diagram with rows one on top of the other. The bottom row indicates the number of producers at the bottom of a particular food chain in a habitat; the next row indicates the number of primary consumers, and so on. The width of the row represents the number it contains.

4 a A is a pooter; B is a pitfall trap.

b To use the pooter you select the organism you are going to catch.

c You can sample organisms that are not on the ground. The sampling process is much quicker than having to wait for animals to enter a trap.

5 a Population size is the total number of organisms; population density is the number of organisms per m^2.

b $3 \div 100 = 0.03$ snails per m^2.

c The environment particularly favourable to certain animals might be in small patches (e.g. dark and damp areas for woodlice).

6 a Animals that don't move very fast.

b 72% (count whole and half squares of grass).

c 28%.

d It is hard to know where one organism begins and the other one ends.

e Take random quadrat samples in a wide range of areas and find an average.

7 a Graph A; the population size is much smaller.

b As the population of rabbits increases there is more food for the foxes so the fox population increases. However, more foxes eat more rabbits, which makes the rabbit population decrease. Then there is less food for the foxes so the population of foxes decreases. This allows the rabbit population to increase again, and the process repeats.

19: Atoms and elements

1 No.

2 Materials are made from combinations of different elements. There is an infinite variety of combinations.

3 Metals conduct electricity; non-metals don't.

4 Mercury.

5 a Symbols are the same in all languages; this prevents problems in communication.

b To distinguish between elements starting with the same letter, e.g. hydrogen (H) and helium (He).

c The symbols are based on their original names, which have subsequently changed.

d i Hydrogen; ii lithium; iii argon; iv sodium; v potassium; vi gold; vii mercury; viii antimony.

e i He; ii Ca; iii Mg; iv Cl; v Pb; vi Sn.

f Helium and chlorine are non-metals; the others are metals.

6 Iron, cobalt and nickel.

7 a Li, Be, B and C are solids; the others are gases.

b Li and Be are metals; C, N, O, F and Ne are non-metals.

c B; a metalloid.

d N and O.

e C.

f It is highly reactive and combines readily with other elements.

8 a They are all reactive metals and their oxides are alkaline.

b They get more reactive as seen by their behaviour in water.

c Rubidium and caesium.

d Alkaline earth metals; halogens; noble gases.

20: Molecules and compounds

1 The atoms in the molecule are both the same type.

2 An oxygen atom with two hydrogen atoms attached to it.

3 SO_2 and HCl.

4 Two nitrogen, eight hydrogen, one sulfur and four oxygen atoms.

5 a Magnesium reacts violently with oxygen so you need to have a safety screen to protect you from potential explosions. Magnesium also burns very brightly so you have to avoid looking directly at the flame so that you don't damage your eyes.

b Magnesium oxide.

c Magnesium + oxygen → magnesium oxide.

6 a The salt in the sea water.

b Hydrogen.

c The water molecules.

d Sodium chloride + water → chlorine + hydrogen + sodium hydroxide.

7 There are twice as many oxygen atoms as there are silicon atoms.

8 a C_3H_8.

b C_5H_{12}.

9 a $CO_2 + C \rightarrow 2CO$.

b $TiCl_4 + 4Na \rightarrow Ti + 4NaCl$.

c $Ca(OH)_2 + 2HCl \rightarrow CaCl_2 + 2H_2O$.

d $2H_2 + O_2 \rightarrow 2H_2O$.

e $Fe_2O_3 + 2Al \rightarrow 2Fe + Al_2O_3$.

f $2ZnS + 3O_2 \rightarrow 2ZnO + 2SO_2$.

g $Fe_2O_3 + 3CO \rightarrow 2Fe + 3CO_2$.

21: Mixtures

1 It is a mixture.

2 Atoms in compounds form very specific bonds which determine the proportions that make up the compound. Mixtures don't form these bonds.

3 The compound splitting into its constituent elements. Silver chloride → silver + chlorine.

4 a A mixture.

5 N coolant, fertilisers; O medicine, welding, rocket fuel; Ne lighting; He meteorological balloons; Kr bright lights; Xe even brighter lights.

6 a Lead is a poisonous material and too dangerous to use in schools.

b 250 °C.

c The tin becomes more concentrated.

d Approximately 180 °C.

e It is lower than both melting points.

f It remains molten over a wide range of temperatures so it is easier to work with before it completely freezes.

7 Amalgam: mixture of metal and mercury; alloy: mixture of metals; gel: mixture of solid particles in a liquid; aerosol: mixture of solid or liquid particles in a gas.

8 The particles of the other element get in the way of the bonds being formed.

22: Weathering of rocks

1 Minerals are materials with a crystalline structure that are the building blocks of rock.

2 All of them are, apart from diamond which is a mineral, and peat which is made from plant material.

3 Weathering is the breaking up of rocks. Erosion is the wearing away of rocks.

4 Physical weathering is the breaking up of rock using force; chemical weathering uses chemical reactions.

5 a It expands.

b Water enters the rock and then expands when it freezes, forcing the rock apart.

c A climate where the temperature frequently fluctuates above and below 0 °C.

6 a 25 cm³.

b 3 cm³, assuming that all of the missing water has entered the chalk rather than evaporated.

c $(3 \div 25) \times 100 = 12\%$.

d The chalk.

e Granite is made from interlocking grains, but chalk has lots of gaps in it.

f Granite; chalk would allow the water to leak out.

7 a The rocks expand and contract in the hot and cold temperatures. This continued cycle weakens them and they break apart.

b Plant life (e.g. tree roots) can force the stones apart. This is called biological weathering.

8 a Rain (or snow) passing through the atmosphere.

b $H_2O + CO_2 \rightarrow H_2CO_3$.

c Calcium carbonate.

d The limestone reacts with the carbonic acid and dissolves in the water. The water then flows away, taking the limestone with it.

e Sulfur dioxide can dissolve in water to produce sulfuric acid. This is a stronger acid than carbonic acid and reacts with the limestone much more quickly.

9 Cave formations are formed due to the erosion of limestone. Stalagmites and stalactites come from the reverse of the reaction: calcium hydrogen carbonate back into calcium carbonate.

10 Every time the water freezes, cracks get wider and new cracks are formed. This allows more water in when the process repeats, which can obviously cause even more damage. Eventually the rock is so weakened due to the number of cracks that it breaks apart.

11 They have cooled down and contracted. The contraction forces have cracked the rock.

23: The rock cycle

1 Igneous rocks are weathered and eroded. The sediment is transported to the ocean floor where it eventually changes into sedimentary rock.

2 Magma.

3 High temperatures and high pressures.

4 They are mixtures of lots of different minerals.

5 a The molecules/particles gradually slow down and bond together in regular patterns as the magma cools.

   b Igneous rock.

   c The larger the crystals, the slower the cooling process.

   d Melt some very pure silicon and let it solidify very slowly.

6 a A new layer of igneous rock is formed every time the volcano erupts.

   b Surrounding the regions where lava flows, especially lower down.

7 a Intrusive rocks form underground and so cool down much more slowly.

   b It is less dense than water.

   c It has cooled down so quickly that it has lots of air holes.

8 a Basalt.

   b Granite and rhyolite are silica rich; gabbro and basalt are iron rich (iron is denser).

   c Gabbro is found in oceanic crust (since it is denser); granite is found in continental crust.

9 a Metamorphic.

   b Weathering, erosion and transportation.

   c Sediment.

   d Sedimentary rock.

   e Magma.

   f Uplift.

24: Types of rock

1 Sedimentary and possibly metamorphic.

2 All three types (even metamorphic rock can change into a new type of metamorphic rock).

3 High temperatures and pressures.

4 They have been compacted together with great forces and so they are held together more strongly.

5 a Sedimentary.

   b They are getting squashed into an interlocking structure.

   c Water leaks into the sandstone, evaporates and deposits its minerals.

   d They are produced in a very similar way to the matrix, except that there is room for the crystals to grow larger.

6 a A large earthquake might have folded the rocks.

   b Pressure and heat would have been created in this process.

   c The mineral crystals within the rock alter their structure at different temperatures and pressures (e.g. graphite and diamond). This alters the properties of the rock.

7 a They all contain calcium carbonate.

   b The proportion of calcium carbonate varies.

8 a Marble.

   b It is non-porous and can be split into flat layers.

   c They get smaller and form layers.

   d They have been squashed with the rocks.

   e Minerals are formed from different combinations of atoms bonding together. The same atoms are still there but they have bonded together differently.

9 a The freezing of molten rock.

   b Intrusive igneous rock is formed below the Earth's surface; extrusive igneous rock is formed above the surface.

10 a Igneous.

   b Metamorphic.

   c Igneous.

   d Sedimentary.

   e Sedimentary.

   f Metamorphic.

g Igneous.

h Metamorphic.

i Igneous.

11 Meteoritic rock.

12 Silicon and oxygen are the most abundant elements in the Earth's crust.

13 Small regions are due to localised effects such as heating caused by magma intrusions; large regions are due to large-scale effects such as boundaries between tectonic plates.

25: Heat and temperature

1 Have three bowls of water: one hot, one cold, the other one warm. Place your left hand in the hot bowl and your right hand in the cold bowl. Once your hands have got used to the temperatures, quickly put both hands in the warm bowl.

2 The joule (J).

3 It is a process that impedes heat transfer.

4 The holes contain trapped air, which is a good insulator.

5 It reduces heat transfer in both directions. Hot things are kept hot by reducing heat transfer out of the flask. Cold things are kept cold by reducing heat transfer into the flask.

6 The material has to move. Solids can't do this.

7 a 0 °C.

b Some of the water would freeze into ice.

c All of the water will have frozen.

d All of the ice will have melted.

e Boiling water consists of liquid and gas at the same temperature.

f Place the thermometer in the ice/water mix and mark 0 °C, then place the thermometer in boiling water and mark 100 °C. Then divide the scale into 100 equal parts.

8 It comes from the bonds being made (particles lose potential energy).

9 The rate that heat is transferred depends on the temperature difference. When the coffee is hot, lots of heat is being emitted so it cools down quicker than when it is cold.

10 a Kinetic energy.

b Particles at the hot end have more kinetic energy than those at the cold end.

c All of the particles have the same kinetic energy (on average).

d The particles have collided with each other, passing on their kinetic energy.

11 a It stops the ice floating to the top.

b Water is a very poor conductor of heat.

c The heat energy would transfer through the copper to the bottom.

12 a A convection current is set up by the candle. The smoke moves with the falling colder air.

b The smoke rises.

c Convection.

13 Conduction and convection need particles. Space is a vacuum so heat transfer from the Sun can't be from these two methods.

14 They have free electrons which can move easily through the metal, colliding as they go.

15 They trap a layer of air, stopping it from convecting. Air is a very poor conductor of heat.

26: Magnetism

1 Cobalt, nickel and iron oxide are magnetic; the other materials aren't.

2 N and S attract; N and N repel; S and S repel.

3 It points due north if suspended from a piece of string.

4 A magnet has N and S poles; a magnetic material is simply attracted to a pole of a magnet.

5 It is a material that reduces the magnetic field. Surround the spaceship with a magnetic material.

6 Magnets: A, C, D; magnetic materials: B, E; not magnetic: F.

7 a A is slightly magnetised; B is fully magnetised; C is unmagnetised.

  b Once all the domains point the same way, you can't make the effect any stronger.

  c It makes the domains jiggle about and point in random directions again.

8 a It is a region where a magnetic force acts.

  b Towards the S pole.

  c They are closest together.

  d It gets weaker.

  e The S pole of the magnet (since N poles will be attracted to it).

  f It is the same shape as that for a bar magnet with the field lines looping away from the geographical south pole around the Earth to enter the surface of the Earth at the geographical north pole. (In reality the magnetic poles are at a small angle to the geographic poles.)

9 A is a wire wound in a solenoid (spring) shape; B is produced by a straight wire.

10 The Earth's magnetic field exerts a weak force on the domains which makes them line up if gently tapped.

11 The domains in the iron line up with the weak field. Each domain produces a little magnetic field which adds to the total effect.

27: Using magnetism

1 A solenoid of wire and an iron core.

2 Greater current and more turns of wire.

3 Reverse the direction of the current.

4 It quickly loses its magnetism.

5 a An a.c. current continually swaps direction; a d.c. current always goes the same way.

  b It is changing direction.

  c Clamp the spring blade at one end above the electromagnet. The blade springs up when the magnet is off and down when the magnet is on. Therefore the blade vibrates up and down.

  d The paper clip is attracted both to N and S poles. Therefore it doesn't matter if the poles keep swapping.

6 a It is an electromagnetic switch. It is used to allow circuits with a low current to control circuits with high currents.

  b If the electromagnet is on, the switch is pulled down and closes the circuit; if the electromagnet is off the spring pulls the switch open again.

7 a When the current gets too high, the electromagnet becomes strong enough to pull the switch open against the pull of the spring.

  b The electromagnet would no longer attract the switch and it would close again. The switch needs to be permanently open until the fault is fixed.

8 a It switches on.

  b The electromagnet attracts the armature towards it.

  c The contacts are separated, which breaks the circuit.

  d It is lifted away from the gong by the spring.

  e The contacts touch again.

  f The situation is back to how it was in part **a** and the process repeats.

9 Soft magnetic materials lose their magnetism at room temperature; hard materials don't. An electromagnet using steel (a hard magnetic material) would be permanently on, even if the current was switched off.

10 High currents heat up wires. Eventually the copper wire melts and the electromagnet stops working. Superconducting wires don't heat up when they carry large currents.

11 Half of the domains will point one way and half will point in the opposite way, thereby balancing their magnetic fields.

28: Light and reflection

1 The speed of light.

2 Both let light through but you can see objects clearly through transparent material.

3 Opaque materials form shadows, since they don't let any light through.

4 Behind it.

5 **a** Don't look directly into it or at its reflections. Put a warning sign that you are using it outside the door.

b The light has to enter your eye.

c The light reflected off the liquid droplets of deodorant into their eyes.

d A straight line.

6 **a** You see the objects inside the shop and also your reflection.

b You don't see any reflections.

c You would see the insides of the shop more brightly.

7 **a**

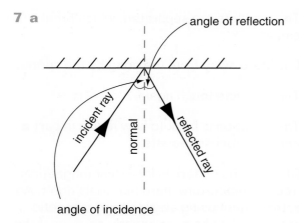

angle of reflection
incident ray
normal
reflected ray
angle of incidence

b They are always equal.

c 120°.

8 **a** 20 cm.

b Left and right are swapped. An inverted image would be upside down as well.

c CHICK is reflected but it is symmetrical so it looks the same.

9 **a** 180°; they are like a single, flat mirror.

b 7.

c An infinite number.

d Each image gets slightly dimmer since the mirror absorbs energy. Eventually the images will become too dim (and too far away) to see.

10 You can't capture it on a screen. Light seems to be coming from it but doesn't actually.

11 3×10^8 m/s. A light-year is the distance that light travels in a year.

29: Refraction and colour

1 It is the changing of direction of light due to a change in speed.

2 Dispersion.

3 Primary colours are pure colours. Secondary colours are equal mixtures of two primary colours.

4 The dye in the jeans reflects blue light but absorbs all the other colours.

5 **a**

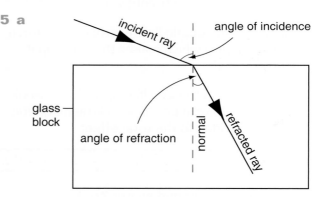

incident ray
angle of incidence
glass block
angle of refraction
normal
refracted ray

b It also reflects a little.

c It slows down.

d The angle of refraction is smaller than the angle of incidence.

e The ray is going along a normal line (they are both at 90°).

6 The rays leaving the surface of the pool bend outwards and look as though they have come from higher up than the bottom.

7 a Different colours travel at different speeds and so refract by different amounts.

b The visible spectrum.

c He masked off all of the other colours apart from green and made the light go through a second prism. There was no further dispersion.

8 The middle is white; red and green give yellow; red and blue give magenta; blue and green give cyan.

9 They absorb the green light and reflect the blue light.

10 Red: red, black, black, red, black, red.
Blue: black, blue, black, black, blue, blue.
Green: black, black, green, green, green, black.
Yellow: red, black, green, yellow, green, red.
Cyan: black, blue, green, green, cyan, blue.

11 Compound yellow is red and green light. Pure yellow is the colour produced in the visible spectrum.

12 Black.

13 Our eyes detect red, green and blue light only (with some overlap). Pure yellow light equally stimulates the red and green cells since this colour lies between red and green in the visible spectrum. Another way of stimulating these cells in the same way is to shine equal amounts of red and green light.

30: Sound waves

1 They are carried by vibrating particles.

2 The speed of sound is fastest in solids and slowest in gases.

3 It is the number of vibrations per second. The unit is hertz (Hz).

4 It is bigger.

5 a They vibrate.

b Make the string shorter or tighter.

c They have different thicknesses.

6 a A.

b B and C.

c Very loud and low.

d A and B.

e C is louder than B.

f The amplitude would decrease. Increase the amplification of the microphone (or the volts/division setting on the oscilloscope).

7 a They have the same amplitude and same frequency.

b Their shapes would be different.

8 a Vibrating particles of water collide with the rubber sheet making it vibrate. The sheet collides with air, making the air particles vibrate, and these collide with each other making the vibrations pass along the tube.

b It focuses the energy into a smaller space.

c Backwards and forwards (rather than up and down).

d The sound waves reflect at the surface of the water back into the water, so hardly any energy is transmitted into the air.

9 a The particles in solids are held closer so the vibrations can pass along more quickly.

b The railway lines transmit the sound from a long distance away.

c Water doesn't absorb sound energy as much as air does.

d The seismic waves are the same as the sound waves.

10 The sound reflects from your hands to go just in one direction rather than in all directions.

11 Our ears are more sensitive at these frequencies, so they sound louder even though they aren't. Babies' ears are very sensitive at higher frequencies.

31: Hearing sound

1 20 Hz to 20 000 Hz.

2 The high end of the range gets less.

3 The decibel scale.

4 a Energy gets funnelled in the outer ear and becomes more intense. It gets converted into mechanical energy at the eardrum and is transmitted through the ossicles. The vibration of the stirrup in the oval window allows the mechanical energy to pass to the fluid in the cochlea. Finally the mechanical energy of the fluid gets transformed into electrical energy in the auditory nerve.

  b It makes the sound more intense and it helps in sensing the direction of the sound.

  c Since the amplitude of vibration is bigger more energy is transferred to the fluid in the cochea.

  d It would limit the energy reaching the auditory nerve.

  e Fluid transmits sound energy quickly and efficiently.

  f It allows the membrane surrounding the auditory nerve to have a large surface area.

5 a These vibrations can travel directly to the fluid in the cochlea, by-passing the damaged ear.

  b The auditory nerve.

  c A damaged ear will respond by different amounts to different frequencies. The hearing aid needs to balance all of these frequencies back to normal levels again.

6 a It is the quietest sound you can hear.

  b Their hearing is impaired since they can only just hear a sound that is louder than 40 dB.

7 a 3000 Hz.

  b Alarms ring at this value so that they are easily heard.

  c The whole graph will move upwards and the higher frequency end will move up still further.

32: Inheritance, variation and selection

1 They are the sex cells that join together in fertilisation.

2 Sperm have tails that enable them to swim and lots of mitochondria to give them energy; egg cells have a lot of cytoplasm to feed the embryo until it is capable of feeding from the mother.

3 They are sequences of DNA that define a particular characteristic and found in the nucleus of a cell.

4 Half of your genome comes from each parent. Less than half comes from a particular grandparent.

5 It is both. Availability of resources such as water, light and minerals will affect tree growth but there are also shorter and taller varieties of tree.

6 a One gamete comes from the father and one comes from the mother. The genetic information from both gametes forms the new individual.

  b They might have inherited the same genes for certain characteristics but different genes for others.

  c Identical twins are formed when a fertilised egg splits into two and each new cell forms an embryo; non-identical twins are formed when two sperm fertilise two eggs.

  d Yes, if they inherit exactly the same combination of genes, but this is highly unlikely.

7 a It is an organism with identical genetic make-up to its 'parent'.

  b Take cuttings and grow them.

  c The amoeba reproduces by splitting in half. Hence identical genes are passed on.

  d It is a clone of the organism that produced the nucleus.

  e Almost every cell (except the gametes) contains all of your genetic information.

f It is very difficult to carry out without damaging the egg; there are also ethical reasons.

8 The sex chromosomes are called X and Y. Your mother will have two X chromosomes and your father will have an X and Y chromosome. Therefore you will inherit either XY or XX. If you inherit XY you are male; if you inherit XX you are female.

9 a Keep on selecting, and breeding from, offspring that show this trait.

b Resistance to disease.

10 a Take cuttings of the geraniums and grow them.

b Clones have identical characteristics that would not change over generations.

c Encourage geraniums with different characteristics to reproduce. Select offspring with features you want and encourage those to reproduce and so on.

11 a Both involve changing the genetic make-up of the offspring to enhance a characteristic. GM crops have had their genes manipulated directly.

b GM crops might reproduce with other crops, with unknown consequences for the ecosystem.

c Improved food yield; increased resistance to disease.

33: Health, diet and drugs

1 Being fit means you return back to normal quickly after exertion; being healthy means you haven't got any diseases and your body is functioning normally.

2 Glucose + oxygen → water + carbon dioxide (+ energy); $C_6H_{12}O_6 + 6O_2 \rightarrow 6H_2O + 6CO_2$.

3 Glucose originally comes from food and is extracted through the digestive system; oxygen comes from the air which is absorbed by the lungs. Both are transported by the bloodstream (pumped by the heart) to the cells where respiration takes place. The waste products dissolve in the blood and are pumped to the lungs by the heart. They pass through into the air and are breathed out.

4 Both involve bursting blood vessels. A stroke is in the brain but a heart attack is in the heart.

5 Carbohydrates, protein, fats, vitamins, minerals.

6 Diets with too much fat; not enough exercise. Changes in lifestyle have led to the popularity of fast food and easy meals. Modern entertainment is produced by computer games rather than active sports.

7 It impairs your judgement and reaction times leading to you taking unnecessary risks.

8 Addiction is the physical and/or psychological dependence on a drug. Tolerance is how much drug is needed before it has the desired effect.

9 a The heart.

b The transport of oxygen is not efficient.

c The vessels have a smaller cross-sectional area and resist the flow of blood more.

d They might rupture.

10 a Smoke contains the drug nicotine.

b They propel mucus up the airways to the mouth where the mucus is swallowed.

c The mucus moves down into the lungs and needs to be coughed out.

d The alveoli become damaged, reducing the surface area of the lungs; air passages become inflamed and therefore narrower.

e Cancer.

f Carcinogenic chemicals can pass from the mother's bloodstream through the placenta into the fetal bloodstream.

11 a It respires anaerobically. Glucose breaks down and releases energy in the absence of oxygen. One of the by-products is lactic acid which leads to pain in the muscles.

b Your body needs oxygen to convert the lactic acid into other harmless substances.

1 *Synthesis* means joining together and *photo* means light, so the reaction is the joining together of carbon dioxide and water through the action of light.

2 Oxygen: relights a glowing splint; carbon dioxide: turns limewater milky; starch: turns iodine solution blue/black.

3 Photosynthesis is the reverse reaction of respiration.

4 It is the total mass of living organisms.

5 a Carbon dioxide + water (+ energy) → glucose + oxygen; $6CO_2 + 6H_2O$ → $C_6H_{12}O_6 + 6O_2$.

   b Light.

   c It lowers the energy needed to make the reaction happen.

6 a Water and carbon dioxide.

   b The tree takes minerals from the soil.

7 a So that you can test whether photosynthesis takes place during your experiment instead of before it.

   b It gets used up in respiration.

   c The iodine can't penetrate the cell walls.

   d Boiling the leaves breaks the cells walls; the ethanol dissolves the chlorophyll and removes the green colour from the leaf.

   e In a water bath.

8 a It is dissolved in the water.

   b Measure how much oxygen is produced in a certain time for different light intensities.

   c Temperature (the rate of photosynthesis depends on temperature); amount of pondweed (more pondweed – more oxygen).

   d You could leave the experiment for long periods of time and continually collect data.

   e The graph will rise with a positive gradient as light intensity increases but then become a straight horizontal line when the rate of photosynthesis is limited by other factors.

9 The plant is respiring and photosynthesising at the same rate.

10 It reacted with other chemicals (particularly iron) and it also dissolved in the water.

11 Oxygen cannot be in an atmosphere of its own accord – it is too reactive. Other process (such as life) must be putting it there.

1 The light energy reaches the tops of the leaves rather than the bottom so this is where photosynthesis takes place.

2 To collect as much light and carbon dioxide as possible.

3 They have a collection of tissues and they perform a specific task.

4 Water is a reactant in photosynthesis.

5 a It is a leaf that has areas containing chlorophyll and areas that don't.

   b De-starch the plant, then let it photosynthesise for a few days. Boil the leaves and remove the chlorophyll using warm ethanol. Finally apply iodine solution. The iodine should turn blue/black where the leaves were originally green, showing the variegated pattern.

6 a They provide the cells with water.

   b They take in the air to provide the carbon dioxide. This isn't needed during the night.

   c They store the gases in the air.

   d This prevents water escaping since it would evaporate too quickly in hot temperatures.

   e So that it is easy for the carbon dioxide to reach the top of the leaf.

7 a So that it can be stored (starch is insoluble).

   b Animals eat the fruits and spread the seeds via movement and excretion.

c They come from the minerals absorbed by the roots. Amino acids form proteins.

d The cell wall.

e To control the passage of chemicals to and from the cell.

8 a The hairs give it a large surface area with which to absorb water.

b They don't photosynthesise since there is no light in the soil.

c From the air trapped in the soil.

d To produce vital materials, e.g. nitrogen for proteins.

e The active transport needs energy; diffusion is a natural effect.

9 The xylem transports water from the roots to the leaves; phloem transports minerals and sugars up and down the plant. The blood supply is used to transport chemicals in the human body.

10 Carnivorous plants obtain their minerals from insects.

36: Metals and acids

1 On all of it apart from a small part on the right-hand side.

2 Mercury; no.

3 Iron, cobalt and nickel.

4 Hydrogen.

5 a They are shiny.

b The atoms are packed closer together.

c A crystal is a regular array of atoms; polycrystalline means they have lots of crystals.

d Metals are much better at conducting heat.

e No, although they all conduct better than non-metals. Graphite is a non-metal that conducts electricity.

f They are strong; they are dense and so relatively heavy.

6 a It reacts violently.

b Hydrogen; gives a squeaky pop in the presence of a glowing splint.

c By evaporation.

d Sodium chloride.

7 a i $Zn + H_2SO_4 \rightarrow ZnSO_4 + H_2$;
  ii $Zn + 2HCl \rightarrow ZnCl_2 + H_2$.

b Salts.

c Water.

d The water makes the hydrogen atoms (ions) separate from the rest of the atoms in the acid.

8 a Potassium sulfate.

b Add potassium to some sulfuric acid. Then evaporate the water – the potassium sulfate should crystallise out.

c $2K + H_2SO_4 \rightarrow K_2SO_4 + H_2$.

9 Metal + acid $\rightarrow$ salt + hydrogen.

10 There is only one form of zinc chloride whereas you can get CO and CO_2 so you need carbon dioxide to distinguish it from carbon monoxide.

11 a It is the maximum possible amount you can obtain if everything works perfectly.

b The sulfate adds to the mass.

c $\frac{2}{3} \times 12.6 = 8.4$ g.

d The two reactants always react in the same proportion. There is only enough sulfuric acid to react with 3 g of sodium.

37: Reactivity of metals

1 It isn't very reactive and so other metals are very likely to displace it from its compounds.

2 The surface gradually becomes duller due to chemical reactions with the air.

3 It is much easier to extract bronze (an alloy of tin and copper) from rocks than iron.

4 Iron oxide. Iron reacts with oxygen (using salty water as a catalyst). It is a problem as rust easily erodes away leaving fresh iron to react with the air. Therefore iron structures gradually become thinner and weaker if they are allowed to rust.

5 a Sodium is a very reactive metal; gold hardly reacts at all.

 b The reaction with the air only happens at the surface.

6 a Concentration of hydrochloric acid and temperature.

 b Magnesium at the top and copper at the bottom.

 c Hydrogen; see if a lighted splint gives a squeaky pop.

 d See how much gas is produced in a given time. The metal that produces the most gas is reacting quicker and is more reactive.

7 a Li, Na, K.

 b Li – bubbles; Na bubbles vigorously and moves around on the surface of the water; K bubbles very vigorously and produces a flame.

 c Hydrogen; it is highly flammable.

 d Put some indicator in the solution and observe the colour.

 e K, Na, Li.

 f Rubidium and caesium; it is far too dangerous.

 g They are very reactive so combust easily. Their reaction with water is violent and would make the situation far worse.

 h It is less reactive.

 i Reactivity increases as you go down the group.

8 a The metal is reacting with oxygen to form a metal oxide.

 b Metal + oxygen → metal oxide.

 c It is more reactive.

 d No chemical reaction takes place.

9 It is shiny so can be seen easily; it doesn't dissolve in water so remains in the pan; it is dense so it sinks to the bottom of the pan; it is not reactive so is found as an element rather than a compound.

10 Place different metal electrodes in a salt solution. There is a small voltage between them. The bigger the voltage obtained, the bigger the difference in their reactivity.

38: Acidity in the environment

1 It is rain that is more acidic than it would be from natural effects.

2 This is the breaking up of rocks due to physical, chemical and biological processes.

3 Soils contain many tiny rock fragments that separated from rocks due to weathering.

4 Lichens don't like acidic conditions. Traffic fumes can cause acid rain.

5 a Carbonic acid, sulfuric acid and nitric acid.

 b Respiration of plants and animals.

 c Volcanoes emit sulfur dioxide.

6 a Carbon monoxide.

 b The carbon dioxide produced can cause acid rain.

 c Nitric acid must be more acidic than carbonic acid since it obviously does more damage (otherwise there would be no point in using the catalytic converter).

7 a Erosion is the wearing away of a material; corrosion is specifically the wearing away of materials due to chemical attack.

 b The product of its reaction (calcium hydrogen carbonate) is soluble and so is easily eroded.

 c Big cities produce more acidic rain due to air pollution. High temperatures speed up the chemical reactions.

 d No, since gold is much less reactive.

8 a The plants need the minerals to function properly.

b It is in contact with the plant for a much longer time without draining away.

c It is a base and so neutralises the acidity of the lakes. More acid rain falls, so the lakes become acidic again.

9 a The water draining through the soil.

b From decaying plants and other organisms.

c The water drains away taking the alkaline solution, leaving the soil very acidic.

10 The bacteria can replace the limestone that has eroded away.

11 The type of vegetation present (some decays into more acidic compounds than others); the types of minerals in the local rocks (with differing pH values); the structure of the soil – as in question **9**, soils that drain easily are often acidic.

12 We are more aware that acid rain is a problem and we are trying to control emissions.

39: Air pollution and global warming

1 Since the Industrial Revolution there have been huge emissions of pollutants into the environment.

2 Global warming is the gradually increasing temperature of the planet. Climate change is a change in the weather possibly brought on by global warming.

3 It reduces the heat radiation leaving Earth in the same way that a greenhouse reduces heat radiation leaving its interior.

4 They are running out and are very useful for producing other materials.

5 a Oxygen.

b It stops the UV light from harming us and other organisms.

c They have damaged the ozone layer.

d In aerosols.

e The CFCs are still present in the ozone layer and they are not biodegradable.

6 a CO.

b It prevents oxygen from attaching to the haemoglobin and so we quickly die through oxygen starvation.

c You can't smell or see carbon monoxide.

7 It is a smoky fog. Laws have been made to reduce the amount of pollution in sensitive areas.

8 a So that the pollutants are released high up in order to dissipate effectively.

b No; the same amount of pollution is emitted.

c Opposite charges attract, so the soot collects on the positive plates. A hammer then hits the plates and the soot falls off to be collected at the bottom of the chimney.

9 a It is waste that can be broken down into harmless chemicals by bacteria.

b It doesn't pollute the environment for as long as conventional waste.

10 a They let the heat radiation from the Sun through them but they reflect the heat radiation from the Earth back down to the surface.

b Yes; most of the greenhouse effect is due to water vapour. It is an essential feature of the Earth's climate since temperatures would be too low for most life forms without it.

c We have monitoring stations high up in the atmosphere (e.g. Mauna Loa in Hawaii).

d Water expands in higher temperatures; land-locked ice melts and drains into the sea.

e The scientists can get primary data about the relationship between global temperatures and carbon dioxide levels.

f The temperature is changing all the time by much more than 0.6 degrees, so they had to make sure they were getting a true average.

11 No, they won't. When an ice cube melts, the water level remains the same. This is because the volume of ice below the waterline gets less as the ice melts, by exactly the same amount as the melted ice added to the water.

12 For example, the Sun's activity, changes in the Earth's orbit.

13 It is an ocean current which moves warm water across the Atlantic to the north of the UK. If this stopped, there is a chance that the UK climate would cool down.

14 The plants' life processes are triggered by changes in the climate. If animals that eat the plants arrive later than the fruits and nuts produced by plants, their food supply could diminish.

40: Energy and electricity

1 Chemical energy transforms into electrical energy.

2 Connect ammeters in series, and voltmeters in parallel across the component being tested.

3 It is the potential difference or the energy transformed per unit charge.

4 An energy transformation is energy changing from one form to another. Energy transfer is the change of location where the energy is having an effect – waves are a good example of energy transfer.

5 a Electrical to kinetic.

  b Sound to electrical.

  c Electrical to heat.

  d Light to electrical.

6 a The total energy before and after any action must be the same – although it can be in different forms.

  b Into heat, which eventually dissipates out into space.

7 a A has used 100 J and B has used 40 J.

  b B is the most efficient since it produces the same amount of useful energy but wastes less.

8 a It is a flow of electric charge.

  b None.

  c 0 V.

d i 2.0 V; ii 2.0 V; iii 1.0 V; iv 1.0 V; v 0 V.

e i 0.67 V; ii 1.33 V.

9 a From chemical reactions in the potato.

  b The chemical reactions no longer have enough reactants.

  c You need metals of different reactivity to create a potential difference (voltage).

  d Potassium is highly reactive with water and therefore too dangerous.

10 The electric charges have electrical potential energy. The voltage is a measure of the difference in potential energy of the charges. It remains at 2 J until it gets to B. It then transforms 1 J into light and heat at the left-hand light bulb so it is left with 1 J at C. It delivers the rest of its energy to the right-hand light bulb so it has 0 J at D. It then remains at 0 J until it gets to E.

41: Electricity and modern life

1 It doesn't run out but appliances can't be portable.

2 230 V.

3 When you wanted a very dim source of light – e.g. a night light.

4 a The energy from a primary fuel has been used to make the electricity; the electricity itself is used to provide energy and so is acting as a fuel.

  b It can easily be transformed into many different useful forms of energy.

  c It is easy to transport.

5 a 60 A.

  b Some of the current is leaking to the Earth, which indicates a fault.

  c They are in parallel – otherwise, if one socket wasn't being used, none of the others would work.

  d It is measuring the electrical energy that you are using.

6 a 4 kWh are used, so the cost is 40p.

b 100 W = 0.1 kW, 20 minutes = 0.33 hours, so energy used = 0.1 × 0.33 = 0.033 kWh.

7 a Electrical energy into light and heat.

b The joulemeter clicked faster.

c This light bulb is brighter and so transforms more energy in a given time. Therefore the joulemeter clicked faster.

d Power is the rate of transformation or transfer of energy; that is, how much electrical energy transforms into light and heat every second.

e The joulemeter would click more slowly since less energy is transformed into heat.

8 a Kinetic energy into electrical energy.

b It amplifies the magnetic field produced by the magnet.

c Rotate the magnet faster; use a stronger magnet; have more coils.

9 They only want to produce as much electrical energy as people actually need. After an important TV event (such as a world cup football match) everyone gets up to put the kettle on and go to the toilet. This requires a sudden increase of electrical energy (the water companies need electricity to pump the sewage if you're wondering why going to the toilet needs electricity!). Unless the electricity companies are producing the right amount, the system could be overloaded, resulting in widespread power cuts.

10 Power lines can transmit electricity with lower currents if the voltage is high. Low currents mean that the power lines don't heat up as much and are therefore more efficient. An electric shock is due to an electric current flowing through you. Birds don't get shocked because they do not form a complete circuit. However, flying a kite into a power line would give you a shock since the electric current can flow from the power line through the kite and down into the Earth (a circuit is formed since the power station is connected to the Earth as well).

42: Gravity and orbits

1 The force of gravity acting on it.

2 The mass is the amount of matter, which stays the same. Your weight, however, changes if you go into space.

3 It would fly off in a straight line.

4 We are much closer to the Earth.

5 a i 600 N; **ii** 5 N.

b i 5 kg; **ii** 100 g.

6 a The Moon has less mass.

b 100 N.

c A 1.2 kg mass would have this weight on Earth. Six times this mass would have the same weight on the Moon so the answer is 7.2 kg.

7 a The mass is (2400 ÷ 10) × 6 = 1440 kg.

b 32 000 ÷ 1440 = 22.2 N per kg.

8 a Towards it – so upwards but the direction and elevation depend on where you are on the Earth's surface (on the equator during one of the equinoxes it will be vertically upwards).

b It would be pulling you equally in all directions. Since these forces balance out, you would feel weightless.

c The Moon is much closer to the Earth, so Earth's gravity is stronger.

9 a It needs to produce a resultant force upwards. This can only happen if the thrust is bigger than the weight.

b The weight of the rocket gets less due to the burning of the fuel and it also gets less since the force of gravity decreases as it moves away from the Earth.

c It continues at a constant velocity.

10 a Towards the centre of the circle.

b It would fly off at a tangent.

c Friction. The car might not be able to turn as tightly and skid off the road.

11 a Gravity; downwards.

  b It has a horizontal speed which isn't affected by any force.

  c It would travel further horizontally before it reached the ground.

  d It would go all the way round the Earth.

  e The force of gravity isn't as strong so they don't fall as fast.

12 It is larger at the North Pole than at the equator since you are closer to the centre of the Earth.

13 You would fall to the centre of the Earth, pass through and emerge at the other side but gravity would bring you to a halt. Then you would fall back again the other way. Therefore you would oscillate from one side of the Earth to the other.

43: Understanding the Solar System

1 The Earth.

2 The telescope.

3 It contradicted the teachings of the Church.

4 It can see objects more clearly without disturbances caused by the atmosphere.

5 a An orbit above the equator that has a period of 1 day.

  b Communications; they are always directly above the same part of the ground.

  c It circles round the Earth between the North and South Poles.

  d The force of gravity is much stronger.

  e As they orbit, Earth's surface rotates underneath them, so for each orbit they are over another strip of the surface.

  f Monitoring weather; spying.

  g The diagram should show the Earth, one horizontal circle around the equator but a long way out (geostationary) and one vertical circle around the Earth much closer (polar).

  h To collect scientific data about that planet.

6 a The stars rotate about a fixed point.

  b The stars themselves are rotating about this point.

  c It is reflected light from the Sun.

  d They moved slowly relative to the constellations.

7 a If it didn't then the model couldn't possibly be true.

  b He made the planets go in little circles while orbiting.

  c Because the model was no longer fitting the facts.

  d Because it contradicted the teachings of the Church and the argument wasn't powerful enough to alter peoples' belief.

8 a He discovered four moons of Jupiter.

  b We feel gravity pulling us to the centre of the Earth, so this must be at the centre of the Universe.

  c He produced a theory of gravity that was consistent with all of the facts and made sense if the Sun was at the centre.

9 The Sun is orbiting the centre of the Milky Way galaxy, which contains billions of other stars. There are billions of galaxies in the Universe separated by vast distances.

10 Pluto is a lot smaller than people originally thought. There are other Pluto-sized objects orbiting the Sun further out.

11 When the planet Uranus was discovered its orbit seemed to be affected by the gravity of another object further out. By using Newton's equations people worked out the position of the new planet and Neptune was discovered.

12 A supermassive black hole; the motion of objects affected by its gravity.

44: Speed, distance and time

1 Average speed = distance ÷ time.

2 Faster.

3 1000 m; 3600 s.

4 $30 \times 3600 = 108\,000$ km/h.

5 $1200 \div 3600 = \frac{1}{3} = 0.33$ (2 d.p.) km/s.

6 a 36 000 m/h.

   b 10 m/s.

   c 0.2 km/s.

   d 72 m/s = 259 200 m/h = 259.2 km/h.

   e 144 km/h = 144 000 m/h = 40 m/s.

   f 20 m/s = 72 000 m/h = 72 km/h.

7 a 10 m/s.

   b The first bike was in front since the average speed of the second bike must be less than 10 m/s at this point if it continues to accelerate right to the end.

8 I will have walked twice as far so we must meet 4 km away from my house.

9 The time would be too short, so the speed would be too high.

10 a Speeding up.

   b 19.6 cm/s and 39.2 cm/s.

   c No; you would need the distance and the time between the two light gates. (The average of the two speeds you calculated would only be the average speed if the glider was accelerating at a constant rate.)

   d It is an average speed over the distance of 2 cm.

11 a The faster the speed, the bigger the force which turns the metal drag cup against the pull of the spring and moves the pointer to show a higher speed.

   b It measures the speed at a point since it does not rely on a distance and a time measurement.

45: Forces and motion

1 A force from the engine makes the car accelerate.

2 The mass is bigger, so the acceleration is less for the same maximum force.

3 It has more resistance; make your body more streamlined.

4 This is the constant speed that an object reaches when it is falling to the ground.

5 Upthrust is a buoyancy force due to pressure. It does not depend on the motion of the object.

6 a Air resistance.

   b The size of the force is very small.

   c The brakes apply a frictional force that is larger than air resistance.

   d The frictional force from the brake pads is larger than the friction between the tyres and the ground, so the tyres begin to slip.

7 a More.

   b Make the engine produce a bigger force; reduce the mass of the car; make the car more streamlined.

   c Air resistance increases until it is the same size as the maximum force of the engine.

   d No, since the maximum speed depends on the maximum force of the engine which is unaffected by mass. However, a heavier car would take longer to reach its maximum speed.

8 a It accelerates at a decreasing rate until it reaches constant speed.

   b Weight acts downwards; air resistance acts upwards.

   c Weight doesn't depend on speed; air resistance increases as speed increases.

   d Air resistance is larger.

   e They are the same size but in opposite directions.

   f 5 s; 2 m/s.

g i It would reach a lower terminal velocity much earlier (all of the graph would be lower than the line; **ii** it would reach a higher terminal velocity much later (all of the graph would be higher than the line).

9 a Air resistance is bigger than the weight.

b The weight stays the same; air resistance reduces until it is the same as the weight.

c A parachute.

d The temperature would be far too high and the parachute would burn up.

46: Pressure

1 Pressure = force ÷ area.

2 At right angles to it.

3 The water pressure increases.

4 Hydraulic systems use liquids; pneumatic systems use gases.

5 a $10 ÷ (2 \times 1) = 5$ N/cm².

b $10 ÷ (2 \times 4) = 1.25$ N/cm².

6 For example, sharp rhinoceros horn, large camel feet.

7 a Air can compress.

b 40 N/m².

c $40 \times 2 = 80$ N.

d 40 times.

8 a Too high, tyre might rupture; too low, tyre might wear excessively leading to a blow-out.

b This reduces the pressure on a given tyre.

c Flat tyres reduce the pressure on the snow and increase the area in contact with the snow.

d A large radius means that the tractor can cope with rough terrain; wide tyres reduce the pressure so tractors don't sink into the mud so much.

9 a Gas syringe.

b The volume stays the same but the pressure increases.

10 Pressure increases with depth; it acts in all directions.

11 a i Upwards; **ii** downwards.

b Pressure upwards is bigger than the pressure downwards (since it is deeper in the water). Therefore there is a resultant force upwards.